LAURANCE W. LONG

Neoevangelicalism Today

Robert P. Lightner

D0873609

REGULAR BAPTIST PRESS
1300 North Meacham Road
Post Office Box 95500
Schaumburg, Illinois 60195

To my father and mother
who taught me to believe and live
the Word of God

Acknowledgments

Grateful appreciation is extended to the following publishers for granting permission to quote from their copyrighted materials:

BAKER BOOK HOUSE: For material from *The Saviour and the Scripture—A Case for Biblical Inerrancy* by Robert P. Lightner. © 1978 by Baker Book House.

HARPER & ROW, PUBLISHERS: For quotation from *One Way To Change the World* by Leighton Ford. © 1970 by Leighton Ford.

For quotations from *The Worldly Evangelicals* by Richard Quebedeaux. © 1978 by Richard Quebedeaux.

For quotations from *The Young Evangelicals* by Richard Quebedeaux. © 1974 by Richard Quebedeaux.

WM. B. EERDMANS PUBLISHING CO.: For quotation from *The Evangelical Renaissance* by Donald G. Bloesch. © 1973 by Wm. B. Eerdmans Publishing Co.

ZONDERVAN PUBLISHING HOUSE: For quotations from *The Battle for the Bible* by Harold Lindsell. © 1976 by The Zondervan Corporation.

Library of Congress Cataloging in Publication Data

Lightner, Robert Paul.
    Neoevangelicalism today.

    Includes bibliographical references.
    1.   Evangelicalism.   I.   Title.
BR1640.L53   1979   230   78-11426
ISBN 0-87227-067-X

                NEOEVANGELICALISM TODAY
                (Previous title: *Neo-evangelicalism*)
                © 1965, 1978
                Regular Baptist Press
                Schaumburg, Illinois
                Printed in the U.S.A.

Contents

Part III: Difficulties

Part IV: Dangers

Part V: Further Developments

Foreword to the Fifth Edition

SINCE THE FIRST edition of *Neoevangelicalism,* major developments have occurred. The trend toward ecclesiastical compromise and abandonment of orthodoxy has become evident. While right-wing neoevangelicals have tended to hold fast to orthodox theology, left-wing neoevangelicals have openly affiliated with the world church movement, have first questioned and then abandoned inerrancy, and now have become leading advocates of neoorthodoxy. Such a major development within so-called evangelicalism requires careful delineation and exposure. Those holding steadfastly to the inerrant Scriptures will welcome this study and its call to orthodoxy in Biblical theology.

John F. Walvoord, President
Dallas Theological Seminary
Dallas, Texas

Foreword

ALMOST A CENTURY has passed since the famous fundamentalist-modernist debates which began in the last quarter of the nineteenth century. Alarmed by the penetration of German higher criticism, evolution, and a liberal form of postmillennialism, theological conservatives in America rallied to defend the faith. Bible conferences centering in reaffirmation of the doctrines of the inspiration of the Scriptures, the substitutionary atonement of Christ and His bodily resurrection, and the personal, second coming of Christ attracted great throngs. A summary of conservative faith described as "the fundamentals" was a natural outcome of this movement.

From the beginning, the fundamentalist movement was attacked by those who opposed its theology and resisted its criticism of encroaching liberalism. Fundamentalists were charged with lacking love for the brethren, as being anti-intellectual and opposed to progress in Biblical studies, and were described as schismatic and intolerant. The fundamentalist movement had its climax in a series of denominational controversies in which fundamentalists attacked liberal trends. The attempt to purge those of liberal theology failed, however, and fundamentalists for the most part either had to conform to a philosophy of tolerance of theological difference on fundamentals or withdraw and form new communions.

Those who withdrew acted on the principle that separation from those who differed on the fundamentals of the faith was essential for a pure Biblical testimony. Those who remained within their old communions tended to justify their actions by criticizing their fundamentalist brothers. It was evident that a new term was needed to describe the theology and attitude of those who believed in working with liberals and a new program was required to justify their position and declare their theology.

For a time the term *evangelical* was used to describe those who shared the theology of fundamentalism but did not believe in separation from those who differed from them. It became evident, however, that evangelicals were not an effective voice in modern Christianity and needed a new approach if they were to impress and gain a following either from fundamentalists on the one hand or the right fringe of liberalism on the other.

The new term first introduced by Harold John Ockenga was entitled *neoevangelicalism.* It claimed the same theology as old-time fundamentalism, but was an attempt to remedy its deficiencies. It first of all was opposed to separationism. The neoevangelical feels free to work in most Protestant denominations and does not believe in separation from them unless forced to leave. Neoevangelicalism countered the oft-repeated charge of anti-intellectualism leveled at fundamentalism by an emphasis on scholarship and intellectualism and endeavored to meet modernism on its own level scholastically. As against the charge of being antisocial and indifferent to contemporary issues which was often laid at the door of fundamentalism, neoevangelicalism emphasized participation in politics and taking a stand on social and moral issues as a necessary adjunct of neoevangelical Christianity. Neoevangelicals also tended to evade some of the criticism leveled at fundamentalism by becoming one of its critics. By some neoevangelicals, the most extreme kind of fundamentalist controversy was pictured as the norm. Neoevangelicalism was loud in its denial of fundamentalist controversy, and at the same time praised liberal theologians for their scholarship, cogency and relevance. Strenuous efforts were made to attract the liberals and encourage them to listen to neoevangelical presentations.

It is obvious that there is much that can be commended in the neoevangelical approach, and fundamentalism is open to certain criticisms. The question that remains in the minds of many impartial observers, however, is whether the basic criticisms of fundamentalism are universally valid and whether the new approach of neoevangelicalism is after all the Biblical approach. The author of this volume has effectively presented both sides of this discussion. Readers may not agree with every statement, but, if the volume provokes thoughtful consideration of the principles underlying a basic Biblical theology and a relevant Christian approach to modern life, much will be gained.

> *John F. Walvoord, President*
> *Dallas Theological Seminary*
> *Dallas, Texas*

Preface to the Fifth Edition

WHEN I WROTE the first edition of this book in 1959, I was convinced that neoevangelicals and their neo-evangelicalism posed a serious threat to historic evangelicalism and to the fundamentalist expression of it. What was then a threat has since become a sad, sad reality. And because of it evangelicalism is sorely divided today. The front is now more disunited than ever.

Not long after my original book was published, another appeared—*The New Evangelicalism* by Ronald Nash, published by Zondervan Publishing House. Nash not only disagreed with my appraisal of neoevangelicalism and its dangers, but he praised the neoevangelicals for many of their advances. He saw no serious threats from the movement. Later, another book appeared—*The New Evangelical Theology* by Millard Erickson, published by Fleming H. Revell Company. Though not quite as optimistic as Nash, Erickson also gave an acceptable and mildly cautionary nod to neoevangelicalism.

Important as these two books are to the understanding of neoevangelicalism, the two recent ones by

Richard Quebedeaux are even more important. Without doubt Quebedeaux is one of the most popular members of the "new generation of evangelicals." He happily identifies himself as a member of the evangelical left. *The Young Evangelicals* was published in 1974 by Harper and Row. In the book he is critical of the neoevangelicalism of which I wrote. He calls it "Establishment Evangelicalism." In 1978 the same publisher published Quebedeaux's *The Worldly Evangelicals*. In this book he surveys the alarming trends within Establishment Evangelicalism toward the left. In it he admits the danger evangelicals face in becoming too much like liberals. Both of these volumes receive extensive treatment in Part V of this book.

Robert Lightner
Dallas, Texas

Preface to the Fourth Edition

THE ISSUES of the total inerrancy of Scripture and ecclesiastical and personal separation continue to divide Christians. Many who no longer wish to be called fundamentalists but rather evangelicals or neoevangelicals feel there is too much of a stigma attached to the term *fundamentalist*.

The contemporary religious scene has become so confused and complex during the past few years that it is becoming increasingly more difficult to categorize some men and movements relative to their theological position. To be on the safe side, labels must be used cautiously when seeking to make identifications. There are increasing variations and degrees of belief within the broad spectrum of neoevangelicalism. Men, movements and organizations often subscribe to certain things which generally characterize neoevangelicalism, and at the same time they often share beliefs in other vital areas with fundamentalists. One must be careful not to classify all who differ with his particular interpretation of fundamentalism as neoevangelical. Too, while those evangelicals who do not wish to be called fundamentalists hold much in common, they do not all embrace the weak view of Scripture which some do. Much unnecessary damage is done by broad accusations and by classifying all who have certain neoevangelical attitudes with those who no longer subscribe to the total inerrancy of Scripture.

Recent developments at Fuller Theological Seminary call for attention in this fourth edition of *Neoevangelicalism*. This is especially true since Fuller Seminary has been designated by Harold J. Ockenga as the seminary which prepares men in the neoevangelical philosophy. Ockenga is the one who coined the term *new evangelicalism* and who was Fuller's president for some time.

Harold Lindsell, who was at one time a part of Fuller, warned of impending departure for the seminary when he said:

> One of the main purposes for the creation of Fuller Theological Seminary was to defend the old Warfield view of the Scriptures—a view that included inerrancy. About ten years ago the seminary was shaken by controversy over the question of Biblical authority and particularly inerrancy or infallibility. Some members of the faculty and the governing board of the institution resigned. The controversy was not fully settled. The seminary has as a part of its doctrinal platform the assertion that the Bible is "free from all error in the whole and in the part." This was unacceptable to some in the institution and the process of revising the statement of faith began. Sometime this spring the trustees will be called upon to adopt a new statement of faith that omits this assertion from Fuller's creedal commitment. The new statement will be more in harmony with the view of one protagonist in the school, that there is revelatory and non-revelatory Scripture: that which is revelatory has no errors in it; that which is non-revelatory has errors in it ("Whither Southern Baptists?" *Christianity Today*, April 1970, pp. 3, 4).

The predictions Lindsell made in 1970 have come true. This should sadden every Bible-believing Christian. In another recent editorial entitled "Doctrinal Changes at Fuller" in the same periodical, the significant changes in Fuller's doctrinal statement were reported.

> A few years ago Fuller Theological Seminary was rocked by a theological controversy that led to the resignation of some members of the faculty and board. The seminary has recently published its new doctrinal statement involving changes that were at the heart of the earlier controversy. The original statement said that the Bible is "plenarily inspired and free from all error in the whole and in the part. . . (and is) the only infallible rule of faith and practice." The new statement eliminates "free from all error in the whole and in the part." The Bible is infallible in those matters relating to faith and practice, according to the new statement. The former statement committed the school to premillennialism saying that Jesus Christ would return "to establish His Millennial Kingdom." Now it reads that He will come to "establish His glorious kingdom," which permits an amillennial view. A third change has to do with the condition of the unredeemed dead. The original statement assigns "unbelievers to eternal punishment"; the current statement says "the wicked shall be separated from God's presence" (*Christianity Today*, May 7, 1971, pp. 39, 40).

In view of these sad developments it is difficult to understand what some prominent Christian leaders continue to say about Fuller Theological Seminary. For example, Ockenga recently gave his full endorsement of the school in the Seminary Bulletin of January 1, 1971:

> . . . Fuller Theological Seminary is . . . the realization of the vision of men and the challenge of God to perpetuate Christian doctrines derived from centuries of study of the Holy Scripture. The seminary's capital fund campaign is yet another step forward in its admirable record of meeting history and its needs all to the glory of God. . . .

Also, Billy Graham, in the same seminary publication, said:

. . . I enthusiastically support Fuller Seminary as one of the greatest evangelical institutions in the world. I thank God for the hundreds of young men and women who are serving Christ throughout the world who were trained at Fuller . . . I commend the development program of Fuller Theological Seminary to all those who love our Lord Jesus Christ.

My purpose in sending forth this fourth edition of *Neoevangelicalism* is the same as that expressed in the first edition. The prayer of the author remains that the book may serve as a lifeline to rescue the brethren and not as merely a washline to expose the sins of other members of the family of God. Exposing is done, not with any personal animosity or hatred toward those involved, but rather with a deep concern that those involved in these things will see the error of their way.

Robert Lightner
Dallas, Texas

Preface to the Third Edition

SOME OF THE new evangelicals have been led farther away from evangelicalism over the current issue of the inerrancy of Scripture. Others who were originally stalwarts in the new evangelical camp now no longer wish even to be called new evangelical because of the extreme position which some of their brethren have taken regarding the Scriptures. Ronald Nash's contention, in his book *New Evangelicalism,* that the doctrine of Scripture was not an issue with new evangelicals and that they all held to the Biblical and traditionally orthodox position has been demonstrated to be a gross error. The most basic doctrine of Scripture has brought division within the neoevangelical fold, and it is still doing so.

The most recent publication dealing with new evangelicalism has been *The New Evangelical Theology* by Millard Erickson of Wheaton College and published by Fleming H. Revell Company. While the book has much to commend it, unfortunately the author fails to deal with the most crucial issues in new evangelical theology today, namely, the serious differences over the total inerrancy of Scripture and the resultant acceptance of theistic evolution on the part of some. While the book lacks careful treatment of these matters, it does not lack criticism of fundamentalism.

Another crucial earmark of the new evangelical school of thought is the doctrine of separation. Neoevangelicals either completely neglect or tone down ecclesiastical separation from apostasy and personal separation from the world until these are virtually denied. Since the last edition of this volume, there has been little change in this attitude. If anything, there has been on the part of spokesmen for the neoevangelical mood an increased attempt to view certain aspects of the ecumenical movement with more favor and to promote the philosophy which really says that the leaders must become more and more involved with the world if they are going to be able to make the gospel relevant to it. A contradiction of John's words "love not the world, neither the things that are in the world" is becoming more and more apparent in the new evangelical philosophy.

May the Lord receive the glory for the contribution which this volume makes to His own and to His cause.

Robert Lightner
Dallas, Texas

Preface to the Second Edition

THE WIDESPREAD reception of the first edition of this volume has been gratifying. My reviewers in this country and abroad have been very fair even though they have not always agreed with all my conclusions. With very few exceptions, and these did not come unexpectedly, my readers appreciated the fair and objective approach. I owe a debt of thanks to the many who responded so graciously with personal letters.

Since the first edition of this volume, an attempted apology and defense of neoevangelicalism and a vigorous attack on fundamentalism has appeared under the title of *The New Evangelicalism* by Ronald H. Nash. This second edition is not an answer to Nash or to anyone else. Rather, it will include the latest developments and dangers in neoevangelicalism especially as they relate to Biblical authority. Thus the additional chapter on the doctrine of Scripture will flatly contradict Nash's presentation which sought to prove the identity of neoevangelicalism with historic evangelicalism in this area. Nash labored long and hard to associate his new evangelicalism with so-called early fundamentalism or evangelicalism. The evidence is to the contrary.

Contemporary evangelicalism faces some serious trends of weakness and deterioration and some of these are related to the all-important doctrine of Scripture. I have tried to present these trends by quoting men who have expressed them, whether all of those men are self-styled neoevangelicals or not. No doubt some who have been quoted, especially in relation to scriptural authority, will object to the association. My major concern has not been to pigeonhole men or to place labels on them. That is well nigh impossible and without real purpose. What is possible and purposeful, though, is to discern and reveal dangerous trends, which if pursued to their logical end would remove any cause for the existence of evangelicalism. This I have attempted to do.

There are other minor changes and corrections which it is hoped will make this edition even more beneficial and complete than the first one.

Robert Lightner
Johnson City, New York

Preface to the First Edition

A BOOK presenting neoevangelicalism in a definitive and objective way is long overdue. This volume is designed to help meet this need. Fragmentary contributions have been made toward an explanation of neoevangelicalism, but no inclusive treatment has appeared. All other movements in contemporary theology must reckon with this new evangelicalism however much they may agree or disagree with it. No group, including liberalism, neoorthodoxy or any brand of conservatism, can escape this new expression of Christianity. My own desire to understand the relation of this new evangelicalism to the contemporary theological scene has prompted the findings which appear on the pages of this book.

The writer has been cognizant of the possible misunderstanding and injury which could eventuate from this publication. Special care and precaution have been taken, therefore, lest his study contribute to the existing confusion in evangelical circles. This work is altogether different from the writer's *Neo-Liberalism* in many particulars. That study dealt for the most part with unbelievers, whereas in this present study fellow members of the Body of Christ are involved. Any evidence of the works of the flesh on the part of writer or reader could do far more harm than good.

This book does not deal basically with apostates, neoliberals or neoorthodox but with those who formerly espoused fundamentalism but now desire rather to be called evangelicals or neoevangelicals. Their honest claim is that they are not deviating from the historical tenets of fundamentalism but merely trying to avoid the term because of the fanaticism and obscurantism which has been associated with it. These neoevangelicals are brethren in spite of all the differences which may exist between them and their brethren. Since they are members of the Body of Christ, the Church cannot rid itself of them but must attempt to understand them, help them and learn to live with them.

This book is intended to clarify, not camouflage, the new evangelical position and its dangers. Therefore, objectivity and honesty must prevail. The intention is not to slay the brethren with the verbal sword and thus further divide orthodox conservative Christianity. That gruesome task has already advanced too far to present a united conservative testimony of the grace of God to a sin-sick world. The intention, rather, is to inform and alert believers, including those who identify themselves as neoevangelicals, of the trends and dangers of that movement. This is to be a lifeline to rescue the brethren, not a washline to expose the sins and failures of other members of the family of God. Exposing will be done, but it is not done with any personal animosity or hatred toward those involved.

The subject is treated under four broad headings: Developments, Doctrines, Difficulties and Dangers. The chapters are brief in most instances for the sake of clarity and easy reading. Because of the rather extensive use of bibliographical material, each chapter is followed by a page of notes. Grateful recognition is given to everyone whose work was consulted in the preparation of this manuscript. Credit has been given wherever quotations were made, but the author is indebted also for many ideas and suggestions which were given to him by others.

Perhaps it should also be stated that the author does not speak in these pages for the school or the association with which he is affiliated. The opinions and conclusions in this study are personal and should not be attributed to anyone but the writer.

Robert Lightner
Dallas, Texas

Part I

EARLY DEVELOPMENTS

1

Definitions

THE PROBLEM of semantics (the meaning and sense development of words) is the cause of a multitude of other problems. The more complex the theological world becomes, and it is becoming more complex, the more explaining, defining and clarifying will need to be done to accurately portray one's position in things spiritual.

In the days of the apostles the simple yet forceful designation *Christian* was sufficient to set one off as a follower of Christ in His message and ministry. Not long after the apostles left the scene of their labors, and in some instances before they left, individuals and groups who differed with the apostolic doctrine also claimed to be Christians.

From the time liberalism began its divisive work in orthodox circles to the present hour, it has not been enough for a believer to be identified merely as a Christian. Even that term must be explained because liberal Protestantism and Roman Catholicism both claim heritage in historic Christianity.

Many of the early Christians were called *evangelicals* because they lived and died for the "euaggelion" or gospel. This appellation was popular through the time of the Reformation, at which time it seems to have lost its popularity in preference for the term *reform*. This is understandable because reform was the issue of the hour. *Reformer* was the term used to designate evangelicals who were in direct opposition to Romanism. As is usually the case with names, *evangelical* soon became the title ascribed to all those not associated with the Roman system. This situation caused those who were Bible believers to seek a new name. The influx of liberals who were non-Romanist, and thus considered evangelical, heightened this need. The term *fundamentalist* began to be applied to those who held to the fundamentals of the faith as set forth in a publication called *The Fundamentals.*

From that day to this, true fundamentalists have believed the Bible to be the infallibly inspired Word of God and have opposed liberalism and every other system which seeks to destroy faith in that Word. Several years ago it was evidenced that dissatisfaction existed with the name *fundamentalist*. The reason for the unhappiness is largely due, it is claimed, to the association which the name has gained. The dissatisfied have expressed desire to be called evangelicals and represent a new evangelicalism. They believe this disassociation from the name *fundamentalist* frees them from many explanations which would be necessary should they continue to carry the fundamentalist label.[1]

Obviously, by whatever name one chooses to be designated, explanations and definitions are necessary. It is a demonstrable fact that everybody interprets what he hears according to his cultural background. Each definitive word is taken by the hearer and passed through his mental grid. In the process of putting these words through the mental grids, often new and totally different meanings are attached to them, some for good and some for ill. These new meanings either exalt or debase according to the individual's mental process which has been affected by his social environment.

The fact that different meanings are connoted by the same terms to different people must be emphasized if one is to understand the contemporary theological hodgepodge of words, some old and some new. *It must be clearly understood that the real issue is not the name one chooses but the determinative beliefs and valid implications which that name conveys.* This is not to say that a name is not important. Names are important. What it does reveal is the importance and need for clarification of what one believes.

Since terminology is not the issue, time and effort will not be spent quibbling over terms. The issue revolves around the defining of beliefs, attitudes and dangers which are at the heart of neoevangelicalism. Attitudes and motives must be carefully guarded lest peripheral issues should be stressed out of proportion to the real issue. The danger is always present to construct straw men and then stand back and watch them fall by means of the preplanned arguments. This is no time to be occupied with incidentals and unimportant matters. The time is ripe for a candid appraisal of the things which distinguish neoevangelicalism from its contemporaries. The criterion of judgment cannot be fundamentalism but must be the Word of God itself. Satan would delight to disrupt the cause of Christ by getting those who claim to preach Him to manifest the works of the flesh in their attitudes toward each other. Only as the heart is indwelt richly by the love of Christ, and the mind desirous to know the truth and to proclaim it, will any progress be made in understanding the real issue.

Following is a list of definitions and explanations of important terms. These are given to clarify in the minds of the reader what is meant by them as they may be used throughout the text. There are variations and shades of differences within each one. Also, the terms overlap, and some men could legitimately be said to hold to more than one position. A rather obvious conclusion comes from observing the list: the Christian

Church has certainly moved away from the simplicity as it is in Christ.

Conservatism: The position which adheres to the Bible as the infallible Word of God. It is sometimes used as a synonym for orthodoxy.

Evangelicalism: This term is broader and older than the term *fundamentalism* but may legitimately be used as a synonym for it. Its root word is a Biblical one and means "gospel" or "glad tidings." It is attached to each of the gospels and, therefore, denotes more than the good news of deliverance from sin through faith.

Conservative Evangelicalism: Some evangelicals believe the term *evangelicalism* should be prefaced by the word *conservative* because some liberals claim to be evangelical. It does not seem necessary, however, to further clarify the term *evangelicalism* in this way. If and when the liberal uses it, *he* ought to define it because one cannot truly be an evangelical and a liberal at the same time.

Neoevangelicalism (new evangelicalism):

> The new evangelicalism breaks with . . . three movements. The new evangelicalism breaks first with neo-orthodoxy because it declares that it accepts the authority of the Bible . . . He [the new evangelical] breaks with the modernist, however, in reference to his embrace of the full orthodox system of doctrine against that which the modernist has accepted. He breaks with the fundamentalist on the fact that he believes that the Biblical teaching, the Bible doctrine and ethics, must apply to the social scene, that there must be an application of this to society as much as there is an application of it to the individual man.[2]

Fundamentalism: The movement which was born in the early part of the twentieth century in opposition to and as a reaction against liberalism. It strongly reemphasizes the fundamentals of historic Christianity. In addition to other doctrines which were held to be basic and fundamental, the area of conflict centered around: (1) the inerrancy of the Scripture; (2) the deity of Christ;

(3) the virgin birth of Christ; (4) the substitutionary atonement of Christ; and (5) the physical resurrection and future bodily return of Christ. The term was used to designate the defense of these fundamentals when it was first coined and this is the true meaning of it today.

Neofundamentalism: This represents those "who are trying to reduce the Gospel to a narrow, timid, censorious, mind-fettering, soul-stifling, anti-intellectual sectarianism, which wrongfully circumscribes the horizons of revealed truth and departs from the original position of fundamentalism."[3]

Orthodoxy: Right or correct belief is applied to this term. Also, it refers to that which is old and traditional. It is the opposite of heresy. It is not a Biblical term but has Biblical overtones.

> This idea is rooted in the N. T. insistence that the gospel (g.v.) has a specific factual and theological content (1 Cor. 15:1-11; Gal. 1:6-9; 1 Tim. 6:3; 2 Tim. 4:3-4; etc.), and that no fellowship exists between those who accept the apostolic standard of christological teaching and those who deny it (1 John 4:1-3; 2 John 7-11).[4]

Neoorthodoxy: The movement which began early in the twentieth century as a reaction against the optimistic view of man which the liberal had taken. While it is built on liberalism's view of the Bible, it claims to be a return to orthodoxy. It is characterized by an emphasis upon the subjective experience of man as a criterion of truth. Neoorthodoxy is sometimes called Crisis Theology, Barthianism, Theology of Feeling and Neo-Supernaturalism.

Modern Orthodoxy: For want of a better name Hordern in his book *A Layman's Guide to Protestant Theology* referred to the school of thought which seeks to mediate between fundamentalism, liberalism and neoorthodoxy as modern orthodoxy. Its adherents believe that other systems deviate at one point or another from orthodoxy while modern orthodoxy is the expression of true orthodoxy. The movement does not rest upon an infallibly inspired Bible and comes close to neoliberalism in most of its doctrinal beliefs.

Liberalism: "The attempt to give Christian content to the stream of man's general non-authoritative knowledge and to do so by means of a non-authoritative method based on reason, experience, and history."[5] The extreme form of religious liberalism is sometimes called modernism.

Neoliberalism: "The attempt to preserve the values of liberalism while reinterpreting them for a new age and new conditions."[6]

Conservative Liberalism: This kind of liberalism is very much like neoliberalism. Its exponents are not as blatant in their denunciations of historic Christianity as the old liberals were. They take the Bible and its doctrines seriously but deny its accuracy and authority.

Liberal Evangelicalism: This term is identified with the Church of England. It refers there to those who are closer to conservatism and interested in restating old truths to make them more agreeable with modern thought.

NOTES

1. Alfred U. Russell, "In Defense of Fundamentalism," *Central Conservative Baptist Quarterly* (Spring 1959).

2. Harold J. Ockenga, "The New Evangelicalism," *The Park Street Spire* (February 1958), pp. 4, 5.

3. Vernon Grounds, *Old-fashioned Faith and Neo-Fundamentalism* (mimeographed paper), part 2, p. 10.

4. James I. Packer, "Orthodoxy," *Baker's Dictionary of Theology* (Grand Rapids: Baker Book House, 1960), pp. 389, 390.

5. Nels F. S. Ferre, "Contemporary Theology in the Light of 100 Years," *Theology Today* (October 1958).

6. William Hordern, *A Layman's Guide to Protestant Theology* (New York: The Macmillan Co., 1955), p. 100.

2

The Rise of Fundamentalism

CONTEMPORARY fundamentalism may be likened to
an ancient, outmoded ship tossed to and fro by the
moving waves of current theological systems. It is
being forsaken by its espoused friends, manned only
by those who are considered by its enemies as belliger-
ent, unintelligent and naive. Its enemies hope it will be
completely battered by the waves of progress. Only a
few of its devoted friends pray for its preservation
amidst the hostile breakers. Even the term *fundamentalism* is becoming more taboo every day. At the turn of
the present century the term was despised by the liberal and modernist. Many conservatives have now
joined hands with fundamentalism's original enemies
in their dislike for the term and some of its historic
implications. They consider it a hindrance rather than a
help to their prestige. Herein lies the basic reason for
present disunity among conservatives.

There are deep-seated connotations in the term
fundamentalism. It is not just a title ascribed to a few
hard-headed conservatives who refuse to cooperate
with liberals. The term itself contains worlds of
theological, historical and doctrinal implications.

The fundamentalist movement was born in the day when liberalism began to overtake denominational schools and churches with its rationalism and denial of the accuracy and, therefore, the authority of the Scriptures. It was begun by men who deemed it necessary to adhere to the injunction of Jude to "contend earnestly for the faith." In the early days of its history, to be called a fundamentalist meant that you were vigorously opposed to modernism and that you stood firmly on the fundamentals of the faith. To be called a fundamentalist then was something akin to being called a Christian in the early days of the church. It meant being the subject of ridicule, false accusations and hatred. The men who began the movement did not do so to boost their denominational prestige. In most cases it meant the loss of any prestige which they might have had in their churches. Most of them found it necessary to leave their denominations and begin new churches, schools, mission boards and other organizations because of the infiltration of liberalism with all its denial of the Word of God. The lines of demarcation were drawn very clearly in those early days. It was not difficult to detect a liberal; his denials were very candid. Neither was it difficult to detect a fundamentalist; his acceptance of the fundamentals was forthright.

Neoorthodoxy deserves more credit for the confusion in both the liberal and conservative camps than it often receives. Until Karl Barth introduced his dialectical subjectivism, under the banner of a new orthodoxy, the two opposing camps of liberalism and conservatism were distinct and clearly opposites. There was also a semblance of unity within each of the camps before Barth shattered liberalism's optimism and divided conservatism's ranks. Liberals are purported to have returned to an interest in Biblical theology. They take the doctrine of Scripture with a great deal more seriousness and have hesitatingly and superficially repented of their optimistic appraisal of human nature. Because of this "healthy" revival caused by neoorthodoxy, and other factors, some conservatives of the neoevangelical school believe the liberal has been at least partially converted and, therefore, conservatives should proceed with an exchange of theological ideas on the great doctrines of Holy Writ. They feel there is much to be gained through such theological table talk. After all, it is reasoned, the liberal is usually a "scholar," and he might be able to teach the conservative many things about the Bible.

The fallacy of such neoevangelical reasoning becomes evident after a candid appraisal of the liberal's "conversion." Has he really been converted? Does he now accept the Word of God as verbally inspired in its original documents? Does he believe in the complete deity of Christ? The answers to these and other questions on the essentials of the faith will reveal that he has been converted only to a rephrasing of his forefathers' viewpoints.

Basically, liberalism and fundamentalism were the only positions held by the majority of Protestants until neoorthodoxy came on the theological scene. This is no longer true. There are many variations within each of these opposing systems. Also, new systems of thought have arisen so that the clarity of the theological issue has been marred. It is no longer a matter of black and white. Much of the black has been whitened, and some of the white has been blackened. Unity does not exist in either liberalism or conservatism. The conservative Christian can well appreciate the many differences and kinds of liberalism. The liberal has reason and human abilities as his authority. It is perfectly understandable, therefore, that there are kinds of liberalism. Conservatism, on the contrary, rests its authority on an entirely different basis. It accepts the Word of God as the infallible source of authority.

Why then all the disagreement and battling within the orbit of conservatism? It is this area of conflict with which we are presently concerned. The story starts with fundamentalism since this is the movement with which the majority of Christians were identified when liberalism was attacking conservative Christianity. What were the fundamentals then? Who may be called a fundamentalist today? These are questions which must be answered before any progress can be made toward an understanding of neoevangelicalism which is a reactionary movement against contemporary fundamentalism.

Heresy, or deviation from orthodoxy, in the early church was one of the outstanding factors which hastened the need of collecting already inspired books into a canon of Scripture. The New Testament canon combined with the Old Testament canon became the manifesto of the early church. Likewise, the intrusion of liberalism and its deviation from the scriptural manifesto necessitated the establishing and setting forth of the essentials and *sine qua non* of historic, conservative, orthodox Christianity. These essentials which were determinative of orthodoxy or heterodoxy were published as *The Fundamentals* in 1909. Before delving into what the fundamentals were and the interesting circumstances which accompanied the publication of the volumes, it will be necessary to sketch the background and to state factors which gave rise to their publication. This proves to be equally stimulating.

The Attacks upon Historic Christianity

The nature of this study does not require a lengthy discussion of all the forces which were arrayed against Christianity. It will only be necessary to touch briefly upon the major factors which did so much to deaden the life of those who were orthodox and dull the edge of orthodoxy's proclamation. The attacks made upon Christianity during the fourteenth through the nineteenth centuries were from without, like those of the second and third centuries.

Philosophical attacks

The philosophical findings of the fifteenth through

the first half of the nineteenth centuries presented to Christianity its greatest challenge. These discoveries struck at the very heart of Christianity—its authority. Though these philosophers were not originally attempting to destroy man's faith in God and the Bible, the outcome of their work did just that. The emphasis which philosophers such as Hobbes, Descartes, Spinoza and Leibniz placed upon reason and material things caused doubt and distrust to be placed upon the objective revelation of the Bible, which has always been orthodoxy's bulwark of defense. Many other rationalistic philosophers followed. Many of them had at the outset a religious rationalism. Locke, Berkeley and Hume were numbered among them.

It is difficult to present a progressive development of the attacks which modern philosophy made upon historic Christianity. The various philosophies greatly overlap, and a rigid dividing and associating of time periods with viewpoints would be going beyond that which history warrants. It seems best, therefore, to deal with basic viewpoints which affected Christianity irrespective of the precise time periods in which they were held.

Rationalism, as a method or theory of philosophy, has the intellect as the standard or rule by which truth is determined. A rationalist is one who has explicit confidence in reason. He is at war with all authority beyond the mind of man. This view of knowledge has no place for the Bible. Some rationalists recognized the possibility of knowledge coming from areas other than the mind. That which was characteristic of all of them, however, was a confident trust in man. Perhaps unintentionally, yet with a great deal of damage, rationalistic thinkers such as Descartes, Spinoza and Leibniz made the preparations for deathblows to historic Christianity. If man, unaided by any outside help, is capable of discovering and following after truth, then the Bible is wrong because it pictures man as completely sinful and helpless. Obviously, therefore, rationalism as a system of philosophy runs counter to the divine revelation deposited in the Scriptures.

In elevating man and his innate abilities, rationalism hit hard at the Bible; and the Bible was historic Christianity's bulwark. Rationalism in its most ardent form sought to prove that rational knowledge was possible apart from and without the aid of faith or divine revelation. This kind of rationalism is not held by many contemporary philosophers. The contemporary thinker usually admits this early type of rationalism did not prove the possibility of knowledge with its method. Nevertheless, the kind of rationalism described above was a severe attack upon historic Christianity.

Naturalism, which is a philosophical world view, holds that the only certain and reliable means of reaching truth is by its own self-styled scientific method. A naturalist begins, whether he admits it or not, by assuming that the supernatural does not exist. The world and everything in it are explained solely on the basis of natural causes. Philosophers who held this world view believed that truth in every area of knowledge is achieved by the same method which is employed in the natural sciences. The honest naturalist must recognize, however, that the mental processes used by the scientist in carrying out his experiments are not discovered by his senses. Naturalism not only made attacks upon historic Christianity but has continued to the present day as an avowed enemy of orthodoxy. One of the outstanding naturalists was John Dewey, father of progressive education.

A familiar form of naturalism is known as materialism. This view holds that only matter is real and whatever exists is matter. Thomas Hobbes was perhaps the first and greatest modern materialist. Though he was not an atheist, materialists frequently are because the system obviously leads to a rejection of God since He is not made up of physical matter.

The trust in man which rationalism exhibited and the naturalistic and materialistic explanations of the universe were anything but constructive to Christianity. Rather, these and other philosophical attacks were destructive and detrimental because they shifted authority from the Bible to human speculation.

Scientific attacks

Science disturbed historic Christianity by casting doubt upon God's concern for this world and by breaking down the barriers between men and animals. Copernicus, who demonstrated that the universe was vast through his discovery of the solar system, made men realize that the earth and mankind were really insignificant. If God existed, was it conceivable that He would be interested in this speck and its inhabitants? Charles Darwin's theory of evolution made the historic and Biblical view of man appear ludicrous. Rather than viewing man in a fallen, depraved, sinful state, the theory of evolution pictured man progressing to perfection. In Darwin's view there was no necessity for the supernatural. Also, biological miracles were not accepted as factual. This had its effect upon other doctrines as well. If man is not depraved, then he doesn't need redemption; no redemption, no Savior; no Savior, no sacrifice.

While the philosophical and scientific attacks certainly affected Christianity, these assaults were outside the orbit of Christianity itself. The attacks which follow were the natural outcome of an application of humanistic methods to the Scriptures.

Theological attacks

In contrast to philosophy and science, the attacks of theology upon historic Christianity threatened orthodoxy from within. There are distinctive and unique features about the attacks; yet, there is a relation between them.

The human authoritarianism displayed in the rationalism described above did not confine itself to philosophy. Theologians soon began to apply to the Bible what the philosophers and scientists had proposed as the criterion for truth. This application found its most vehement expression in *destructive higher criticism*. This system addressed itself to the Old and New Testaments. The Old Testament representative was Julius Wellhausen from whom the Wellhausen hypothesis got its name. The Wellhausen school completely rearranged the Old Testament. The basis for changing the traditional chronological order of Law, Psalms, Prophets to Prophets, Law, Psalms was based upon an evolutionistic concept of Israel's religion. The new arrangement of books made it impossible to believe in their genuineness and credibility.

The New Testament also was attacked by destructive higher criticism. The Gospels became the first area of attack, and then the Epistles suffered the same assaults. Later dates were assigned to the books so that the Bible-claimed author could not have written the book. Whenever the critic did not want to accept a passage, perhaps because it conflicted with his views, it was simply stated that a later writer, known as a redactor, had made the change. There was a strong denial of the supernatural; hence, miraculous and prophetical elements were considered absurd. The whole doctrine of inspiration was redefined in accordance with the individual critic's viewpoint.

In addition to the philosophical, scientific and theological attacks there were numerous other forces arrayed against historic Christianity. The theological variations from historic Christianity based upon destructive higher criticism are styled variously as modernism or religious liberalism. It was to these various attacks both from within and without that conservative Christianity counteracted.

Early Counteractions of Conservative Christianity[1]

In the face of such hostile opposition, orthodoxy sought to reemphasize its God-given task of evangelism and discipleship. Before the publication of *The*

Fundamentals, men sought to defend the Biblical faith of their fathers which they believed was divinely revealed in the Bible. Their defense took various forms.

Bible conferences

The first conference of great importance was prophetical in nature. It met in 1877 in New York City. Its most outstanding purpose was to enhance the view that Christ's return was to be personal and prior to the Millennium. In the process of promoting premillennialism, it was strongly opposing postmillennialism which believes that Christ will return after the Millennium. Other conferences were held, but the most famous and influential was the Niagara Bible Conference in 1895. This group set forth the famous five-point statement of doctrine. The five doctrinal points were: the inerrancy of the Scriptures; the deity of Christ; His virgin birth; His substitutionary atonement and physical resurrection; and His bodily return to earth. Attending this conference were such men as A. J. Gordon, A. T. Pierson, C. I. Scofield and James M. Gray. The doctrinal issues which these and other leaders put forth, and upon which there was to be universal Christian acceptance, were obviously not considered true tests of orthodoxy by the liberals.

Mass evangelism

As early as Edwards, Whitefield and Finney, revivals were used to reach the lost and carnal with the unchanging message of the Bible. The emphasis which the revivalists placed upon the authority of the Bible served to counteract the criticisms which science, philosophy and religion were hurling against it. These revivalists, and later ones such as Moody, Torrey and Sunday, were criticized not only because of their messages but also because they were "unschooled" and, therefore, uninformed of social advances.

The intrusion of the teaching of evolution and its kindred doctrines into the public school systems, along with the liberalization of theological seminaries such as Andover Seminary, Union Theological Seminary and the Divinity School in Chicago, gave rise to the founding of Bible schools. Notable among them was Moody Bible Institute, established in 1886. The avowed purpose of the Institute was to produce men and women with a passion for souls and thus increase the spirituality of the church in view of the evident advancement of apostasy. The early founders of the school believed that the school had come into existence to oppose the apostasy of the hour. Many other schools followed which had similar purposes and objectives.

The printed page

Periodicals such as *The Truth* and *The Watchword* published by J. H. Brooks were reminders of the nearness of the coming of the Lord. Proceedings of the Bible conferences were often put into print. Weekly journals and brochures found a ready reception with those desirous to defend the old faith. Larger projects were promoted which assailed the liberal's viewpoints. Augustus Strong wrote his three volumes of *Systematic Theology*. James Orr contributed unexcelled scholarship in his publications. Outstanding theological journals such as the *Princeton Theological Review* and *Bibliotheca Sacra* staunchly defended orthodoxy.

Popular preaching

It is true that doctrinal error usually starts in the classroom. But it is equally true that that error is transmitted to the man in the pew by the man in the pulpit. As theological error began to infiltrate the denominations, the conservative saw the need of reemphasizing central doctrines of the faith. Evangelical preachers attempted to refute the higher criticism of the liberals.

They also pointed out the dangers and fallacies of accepting the liberal's view of the virgin birth and the atonement. The social gospel which was being preached by the liberal was attacked tenaciously by the conservative pulpiteer.

These were some of the early attempts to stem the tide of unbelief. Certainly, these and other efforts succeeded, in part at least, in defending the faith. However, there needed to be a concise, detailed and scholarly presentation of historic Christianity. This appeared with great impact and its force is still being felt today.

The Publication of *The Fundamentals*

The story starts with Lyman and Milton Stewart, two Spirit-led laymen from California. These men made possible the publication of *The Fundamentals* in 1909. The set appeared in twelve volumes. The influence of this scholarly defense of the faith was widespread. It was read by friend and foe. Three million copies were circulated, mostly on a free basis. This monumental work not only reinstated and clearly defined conservative Christianity, but it also proved that the position was held by many. James Orr, Griffith Thomas, Arno C. Gaebelein, James M. Gray, Benjamin B. Warfield and C. I. Scofield serve as examples of the caliber of men who contributed the articles.

The work consisted of a defense for historic Christianity, especially in those areas where philosophy, science and theology had attempted to play havoc. "The central figure in the writings of the twelve volumes was the person of the Christ. With rare exception He occupied the preeminent place in every article contributed, regardless of the nature of the subject treated."[2] *The Fundamentals* was published again in 1917, this time in a four-volume edition. In 1958 The Bible Institute of Los Angeles sponsored the third publication in a two-volume set edited by Charles L. Feinberg.

Fundamentalism as a movement started, therefore,

in 1909 with the publication of its manifesto. It produced no new truth but merely reemphasized what historic Christianity always believed. The movement was a reactionary movement without question. From that day to this, what was considered a small, isolated and bigoted movement was given a place in the changing theological world. Its founders recognized an enemy and staunchly proceeded to defeat it. That same enemy has continued to harass orthodoxy to the present hour. Though the leaders of fundamentalism have changed, the movement still exists as a vibrant, reactionary movement. It has not died because its original enemy has reproduced many followers who, in spite of their orthodoxical disguise, are still the avowed enemies of Bible-revealed Christianity. Its enemies are more numerous and subtle, hence, more dangerous. Fundamentalism will not lay down the armor until the enemy has been eternally captured by the King of Kings and Lord of Lords.

NOTES

1. For details of this section and the next one on the publication of *The Fundamentals,* I am largely indebted to Stewart G. Cole, *The History of Fundamentalism* (New York: Harper and Brothers, 1931).

2. Ibid., p. 59.

3

Dissatisfactions with Fundamentalism

LIKE THE YOUNG child who decides to run away from home because he believes his parents are too strict and old-fashioned, many neoevangelical leaders were fundamentalists who became dissatisfied with fundamentalism and decided to forsake its ranks. Not only has neoevangelicalism drawn upon fundamentalism for its leadership, but many of its followers were once ardent supporters of fundamentalism who decided to do what the boy next door did—run away from home. Those dissatisfied with the term *fundamentalism* feel it needs to be placed in cold storage, as one writer put it, until it begins to have a universal meaning for all who use it. Having dealt briefly with the problem of semantics earlier, one needs only a reminder to be convinced that if the term *fundamentalism* is to be in cold storage until it begins to acquire the same meaning for all who use it, it will no doubt freeze to death. That in itself would not be too serious, for words do take on different meanings with the passing of time and cultures. What is a serious likelihood is that with the discarding of the term there may also be the disappearance of the theological implications associated with it.

The exact beginning date of the new evangelical movement is somewhat difficult to determine. The phrase *the new evangelicalism* was coined in an address at a convocation at Fuller Theological Seminary in 1948.[1] The new evangelical approach had begun earlier than this, but after the actual introduction of the term the dissatisfaction with fundamentalism became vocal. The approach is actually an outgrowth of fundamentalism and its controversy with liberalism. It is an honest attempt to remain true to historic Bible-revealed Christianity and at the same time avoid any polemics with the liberal.

It is entirely fitting and proper that probings be made into the why's and wherefore's of the dislike for the fundamentalist label. Why the dissatisfaction? What has caused the unhappiness? Is the dissatisfaction, and oftentimes pure ridicule and fun-poking, valid? Does the new label free the holder from the undesirable stigmas of the old one? Probably the most important question for all of conservative Christianity is, Has the product been changed with the changing of the wrapping? Perhaps one more question is in order, Will the new label provide the opportunity for a different product in the future?

Secondhand resources will not provide the proper information for answers to many of these questions. Recourse must be made to the writings of the dissatisfied and those who prefer not to be labeled fundamentalists.

Carl F. H. Henry, a respected conservative theologian, spelled out several reasons for his dissatisfaction with fundamentalism.[2]

Displaced doctrinal responsibilities

These came, Henry argued, as a result of insistent concentration on the fundamentals. All of the emphasis on the essentials of the faith brought about a disinterest and oftentimes pure neglect of church creeds. Then, too, the peripheral doctrines were not considered in

Corrective theological emphasis

In its vehement opposition of liberalism, it is claimed that fundamentalism became too little concerned with "the whole counsel of God." Christianity was not presented as a world view, and fundamentalists were too otherworldly. They not only failed to deal with Christianity as a philosophy and neglected personal and social ethics, but also cast suspicion upon those who did. Fundamentalists were more concerned with personal piety than the crying needs of civilization. The intellect, Henry continued, was belittled, thus giving rise to unscholarly approaches to the problems at hand.

Lack of theological and historical perspectives

Fundamentalism is accused of surviving on a borrowed academic strength. Rather than a dedication to the task of producing scholarly books, it relied on reprints of the theological classics of bygone days. Fundamentalists were too busy combating the inroads of modernism and carrying on a traditional program of missions and evangelism to bother with theological minutiae.

Tendency toward antidenominationalism

This, of course, came as a result of the divisions between the fundamentalist and modernist. Fundamentalism was not satisfied with nondenominational and interdenominational fellowships but sorely criticized denominationalism. There was not a vital interest in the doctrine of the church except in dealing with the issue of separation.

Emphasis upon premillennial dispensationalism

A premillennialist is one who believes Christ will return before the establishment of the Millennium. A dispensationalist is one who accepts the fact that God has dealt differently with men through the ages and that He has exercised His right to apply different rules of life for different periods in the history and life of man. Henry claimed that fundamentalists identified Christianity too rigidly with this view. He admitted that premillennialism was already present when fundamentalism was born, but that especially after World War I it became largely a premillennial enterprise.

Fundamentalists are accused for not bringing Christianity to bear upon culture and social life.

> When the classic liberal theology was at last overtaken by an inevitable judgment and collapsed, fundamentalism, with its uncompromised regard for the authority of Scripture, saw the theological initiative pass not back to the evangelical forces but rather to neo-orthodoxy, a movement fearless to criticize liberalism in terms of both internal philosophical and external biblical points of view.[3]

A shifted emphasis

Early fundamentalists exerted a positive and profound influence upon the theological world, but that early impact is contrasted with a contemporary temperament rather than a theology. Henry claimed it is no longer a theological position but rather a mood and disposition. Present-day fundamentalism is bankrupt because of the reactionary spirit which it acquired in its vigorous polemic against modernism. Worse than that, fundamentalist leaders were accused by Henry of exhibiting a harsh temperament, a loveless spirit and an unnecessary spirit of strife. The battle was not only waged by the fundamentalist against opposing modernistic organizations and personalities, but soon condemnation was hurled against brethren who were not aligned with separatist movements. The neoevangelical insists that these unhealthy attitudes were not present in the men who wrote *The Fundamentals*.

The above list constitutes the flaws which gave rise to dissatisfaction with fundamentalism for one of the most outstanding neoevangelical leaders, who formerly espoused fundamentalism. When the dissatisfaction first became apparent, Henry and others saw no need of changing the name.

> There is no necessity for abandonment of the Fundamentalist fort, on such secondary grounds, nor for moving to an obscure neo-Fundamentalist position, or to so-called conservatism as differentiated from Fundamentalism; there is already too much terminological confusion, and one always runs the danger of being identified with liberal Fundamentalists who emphasize only the fundamentals of liberalism, and the further danger of encouraging a willingness to be misunderstood.[4]

Ten years of unhappiness with fundamentalism changed Henry's earlier attitude, however, for he later affirmed that essential Christianity need not be identified with either the liberal perversion or the fundamentalist "heresy." "May not evangelical Christianity, dissatisfied with both fundamentalism and modernism, transcend the alternatives of the modern fundamentalist controversy?"[5]

The man who coined the phrase *the new evangelicalism* was Harold John Ockenga. He expressed his dissatisfaction with fundamentalism by summarizing its deficiencies in three major areas. According to him, fundamentalism has a wrong attitude, a wrong strategy and has had wrong results.

The attitude of the fundamentalist is wrong because of an unwarranted suspicion of all who do not hold every doctrine and practice which he does. This suspicion is a result of the personal and ecclesiastical persecution which the fundamentalist has suffered because of his stand for the truth.

The strategy of the fundamentalist is wrong because he believes that you can have a pure church on a local and denominational level. Ockenga argued that this pure-church idea was based on 2 Corinthians 6:17 and 18:

> Wherefore come out from among them, and be ye separate, saith the Lord, and touch not the unclean thing; and I will receive you,
> And will be a Father unto you, and ye shall be my sons and daughters, saith the Lord Almighty.

The results of the fundamentalist are wrong because they have lost every ecclesiastical battle in the historical scene for fifty years. Every major denomination has been lost by fundamentalism. There have been no revivals in the Communist-fundamentalist controversy. The mission fields of the world have also suffered, Ockenga continued, because of the wrong emphasis of the fundamentalist. While fundamentalism has retained the preaching of the gospel and the advance of evangelism, it has not penetrated with its theology into the social problems of the day.[6]

An even sterner critic of fundamentalism and a leader in neoevangelicalism was Edward John Carnell, late professor of apologetics at Fuller Theological Seminary. For Carnell, fundamentalism was a peril of orthodoxy. It was orthodoxy gone cultic. The capital mistake which fundamentalism made was to fail to connect its convictions with the classical creeds of the church. Carnell believed that fundamentalism was only a mentality, not a movement. This grave peril, Carnell argued, was too rigid, too clear-cut in its pronouncements and denunciations. He sharply criticized J. Gresham Machen for taking such an absolute stand on such a wrong relative issue as separation from the Presbyterian Church U.S.A. because of modernists in its agencies. Carnell joined Henry in his criticism of fundamentalism because of its *associations with dispensationalism and its so-called intellectual stagnation.* He was angrily dissatisfied with the *negativism* displayed in fundamentalism, especially in the area of a separated life from social mores. *Fundamentalism elevated evangelism too much* for Carnell. It had more concern for the salvation of souls than charity and the societal impact which it should make upon the world.[7]

In most of the criticisms of fundamentalism, success is evaluated out of proportion to faithfulness. The charge of failure is usually leveled without any consideration of whether or not the fundamentalists have been faithful to God. The degree to which fundamentalism has been successful in changing society is not a valid criterion for judging it.

Honest confession is always good for the soul, even the soul of a fundamentalist. The sincere, truth-seeking fundamentalist will readily admit his own failures and shortcomings and those of his forefathers and brethren. There are shady strands in the history of fundamentalism. In an honest desire to defend the faith, some have denied the love which they owed to the brethren. There have been cases of orthodoxy in doctrine and heterodoxy in practice. These failures are humbly admitted and confessed by many fundamentalists. Criticisms given in the proper spirit must always be evaluated and steps should be taken toward the correction of weaknesses and failures.

A perusal of the dissatisfactions of the neoevangelical leaders will reveal three stupendous weaknesses. *First, they rest on a faulty premise.* The underlying supposition, whether expressed or unexpressed, is the attitude that the war between the modernist and the fundamentalist is over. If not over, at least it is now only a cold war as opposed to the hot war which was waged in the twenties. Speaking of the fact that fundamentalists failed to connect their convictions with the creeds of the church, Carnell made this observation: "Therefore, when modernism collapsed, the fundamentalist movement became an army without a cause. Nothing was left but the mentality of fundamentalism, and this mentality is orthodoxy's gravest peril."[8] The same writer spoke of the "presumed apostasy of the historic denominations."[9] Another speaks of "the marked swing to a greater theological conservatism . . ."[10]

which indicates an optimistic attitude toward the liberal claims of a return to Biblical theology.

The contemporary theological scene does appear to support these claims on the surface. When the meanings and foundations of doctrines are unveiled, however, one is made sadly aware that the liberal has not been converted after all. Granted that some have been converted, the avalanche has not been nearly as stupendous as it is sometimes made to appear. One questions the inclusiveness of statements such as Blaiklock made when explaining the indictment which neoorthodoxy brought upon liberalism. "There were others, and they are world wide, who genuinely returned to a conservative faith and found it satisfying."[11] Anyone conversant with the contemporary scene knows very well that the cold and candid denials of yesterday's liberalism are not being made today. Upon examination, however, of the liberalism of today one finds the same unbelief attractively presented so as to appeal to the religious-minded crowd of the day.

This basic presupposition which the neoevangelical makes is that which causes his unhappiness with fundamentalism, and why should he not be unhappy? If there is no real enemy, why fight? The fact of the matter is, there is an enemy—liberalism—and it is more subtle than ever before.

Secondly, they are too universally condemning. This is a danger which must always be avoided in analyzing a theological movement. No doubt, these weaknesses in fundamentalism are present in the attitudes and actions of some, but they certainly are not characteristic of the entire movement. As the case is presented by the neoevangelical, it is frequently portrayed in broad, sweeping condemnations as though weaknesses were the rule and strengths the exception. One gets the impression that all the contemporary fundamentalists are radicals, unscholarly, anti-intellectual bigots, obscurantists and liberal-haters seeking status in the cult. Occasionally, the neoevangelical will admit the value of the fundamentalist heritage, but only very rarely is any respect shown for the continuing fruit of that heritage in contemporary fundamentalism. Most neoevangelicals fail to distinguish between the essence of fundamentalism and the fanatical accretions of fringe groups.

As an illustration of the latitude of their criticisms, take the one which accuses fundamentalists of being anti-intellectual. Perhaps this criticism comes because the fundamentalists do not adhere to the pseudointellectualism of the hour. The determination of intellectualism is a rather subjective thing; it depends on the one who is evaluating. All too often intellectualism is made to be synonymous with agreement. You agree with me and my views and you are intellectual; if you do not, you can hardly be classified as a learned man. In theological circles the liberal has set the pace for intellectuality. Anyone receiving his training from a school which has not had its facilities and curriculum approved by the liberals' standards set forth by the American Association of Theological Seminaries is not educated. Because the fundamentalist rejects completely any scientific claim which speaks disparingly of the Bible does not mean he does not know of the claims or that he is anti-scientific. Because the fundamentalist rejects any philosophical approach which shows disrespect for the "thus saith the Lord" does not mean he does not know such philosophical systems exist or that he is antiphilosophical. In other words, intellectualism relates to knowledge, not agreement with somebody else's standards. Maybe the neoevangelicals' overly optimistic attitude toward the liberals' "conversion" has caused this respect for the liberals' standards of intellectualism.

Undoubtedly, many preachers and Christian workers who call themselves fundamentalists have done, and are still doing, a service for the Lord without any formal training and education. This certainly is the exception and is becoming less true all the time. God does not put a prize on ignorance; neither does He put one on intelligence which is gained for intelligence's sake alone. An examination of the fundamentalist schools which are listed in the *Education Directory Part III*, published by the United States Office of Education, seems like a fairer medium by which to determine the attitude of fundamentalists toward academic excellence. Men from the faculties of Christian colleges and theological seminaries which strongly favor fundamentalism are producing literature on a high academic level. It hardly seems fair in light of these things to accuse all of contemporary fundamentalism of being anti-intellectual and of belittling intellectualism.

Thirdly, the weaknesses as presented by the neoevangelical often misrepresent the doctrinal views of fundamentalists. A case in point is the doctrine of the church. Neoevangelicals frequently present the fundamentalist as one who believes in the possibility of a pure church. He explains the fundamentalist's view of separation from apostasy by saying that he separates because of impurity and seeks to establish a pure church. The fact of the matter is, the fundamentalist does not believe he has a pure church or ever will have. He rather believes in maintaining pure doctrine as he understands its revelation in the Bible. An intelligent fundamentalist readily admits imperfection in people and churches, but this does not blind him to the scriptural exhortation to "turn away" from false doctrine which destroys the Word of God.

The liberal builds a similar straw man when he pictures the fundamentalist as holding to the dictation theory of inspiration. He accuses the fundamentalist of believing that God dictated the words of Scripture as a businessman dictates letters to his secretary. He then proceeds to blow over his straw-man fabrication by showing the fallacy of such a view. And there certainly are fallacies in the view, and it is easy to disprove it. The point is that it is *not* the fundamentalist's view of the inspiration of Scripture, and the liberal knows it.

The real view of the fundamentalist, which is supported by the Bible, is not so easily overthrown, however. This is why the liberal imposes a different view on the fundamentalist. It seems as though this is what the neoevangelical is also doing to the fundamentalist in the doctrine of the church.

Take as another example of misrepresentation the neoevangelical's criticism of the fundamentalist's lack of interest in social life. In spite of honest efforts and accomplishments of social endeavor at home and abroad, neoevangelicalism harshly criticizes fundamentalism. While it is true that fundamentalism needs more concern for social problems, it ought not be implied that it has no concern. Fundamentalists are concerned, but societal ills are not their first interest.

Much benefit can be had from these evaluations of fundamentalism by those who themselves were once labeled fundamentalists but now wish to be called new evangelicals. The fundamentalist must face these honestly and profit from past mistakes. He needs to carefully present his attitudes and actions toward those that differ and those who are without.

NOTES

1. Ockenga, "The New Evangelicalism," p. 7.

2. Carl F. H. Henry, *Evangelical Responsibility in Contemporary Theology* (Grand Rapids: Wm. B. Eerdmans Publishing Co., 1957), pp. 32-47.

3. Ibid., p. 36.

4. Carl F. H. Henry, *The Uneasy Conscience of Modern Fundamentalism* (Grand Rapids: Wm. B. Eerdmans Publishing Co., 1947), pp. 62, 63.

5. Henry, *Evangelical Responsibility,* p. 32.

6. Ockenga, "The New Evangelicalism," pp. 5, 6.

7. Edward John Carnell, *The Case for Orthodox Theology* (Philadelphia: The Westminster Press, 1959), pp. 113-126.

8. Ibid., pp. 113, 114.

9. Edward John Carnell, "Orthodoxy: Cultic vs. Classical," *The Christian Century* (March 30, 1960), p. 377.

10. Henry, *Evangelical Responsibility,* p. 51.

11. E. M. Blaiklock, "Conservatism, Liberalism and Neo-orthodoxy: A Present-day Survey," *Eternity* (August 1960), p. 27.

4

Proposed Solutions

THE UNHAPPINESS and dissatisfaction with fundamentalism warrant some substitute program of improvement. This chapter will deal with the ways by which the neoevangelical is seeking to correct the errors of his forefathers and foster brethren who identify themselves with contemporary fundamentalism. The present status of the neoevangelical position will also be presented.

The proposed solutions to do what the fundamentalists failed to do or erred in doing are many. They will be presented objectively as they are given by the neoevangelical without any detailed evaluations, which will be reserved for a later chapter.

Disown the Modernist Perversion and the Fundamentalist Reduction of Biblical Theology[1]

The new evangelicalism finds it necessary to reject the two extremes of modernism and fundamentalism in its search for the evangelical imperative. Modernism was proven inadequate because of its unbelief, and fundamentalism is bankrupt because of its mentality and reactionary spirit. Fundamentalism, it is argued, has reduced itself from a theology to a temperament, from a mood to a mentality. This determination to break with fundamentalism was expressed early in the history of the neoevangelical movement. The early leaders clearly expressed this objective not only in relation to fundamentalism; they were desirous also of breaking with neoorthodoxy and modernism.

The new evangelicalism breaks with neoorthodoxy because it accepts the authority of the Bible as a plenarily inspired Bible which is historically trustworthy and authentic. The new evangelical breaks also with the modernist because he embraces the full orthodox system of doctrine as opposed to that which the modernist accepts. He breaks with the fundamentalist in that he believes the Biblical teaching must apply to the social scene as well as to the individual man.[2] The neoevangelical wants to be distinguished from the fundamentalist in areas of intellectual and ecclesiastical attitude.[3]

It is argued that this desire to turn away from fundamentalism is not with any intention of turning away from traditional fundamentalism but only from the mentality which is expressed in contemporary fundamentalism. Neoevangelicals have no present inclinations to forsake the traditional fundamentals of the faith, but they are inclined to disavow what they consider the inadequate scriptural content and disrepute of fundamentalism. Thus, they are turning away from the term. The expressed desire on the part of neoevangelicalism is to divorce itself from the stigma which the contemporary fundamentalist temperament has acquired and at the same time remain wedded to the theological formulations and unchanging realities of fundamentalism.

Bring Orthodox Christianity To Bear upon the Theological Confusion of the World

The general objectives or solutions, which are to correct the failures of fundamentalism, were presented in an article by Harold John Ockenga:

The evangelical has general objectives he wishes to see achieved. One of them is a revival of Christianity in the midst of a secular world. . . . The evangelical wishes to retrieve Christianity from a mere eddy of the main stream into the full current of modern life. He wishes to win a new respectability for orthodoxy in the academic circles by producing scholars who can defend the faith on intellectual ground. He hopes to recapture denominational leadership from within the denominations rather than abandoning those denominations to modernism. He intends to restate his position carefully and cogently so that it must be considered in the theological dialogue. He intends that Christianity will be the mainspring in many of the reforms of the societal order.[4]

In order that orthodoxy may have relevance in the contemporary scene, the neoevangelical insists that evangelicalism must align itself with the current cry for a return to Biblical theology. The plea for a Biblical theology on the part of the liberal and neoorthodox must be received with enthusiasm. Evangelicals, it is contended, must not react against or resist the neoorthodox Christocentric phrasing of revealed theology and his new emphasis on the witness of Scripture to the Word of God. The neoevangelical grants that there are weaknesses in the contemporary liberal and neoorthodox views but at the same time warns against depreciating the strength, concern and courage of those views. The conservative is called upon to welcome the neoorthodox as friends and brethren. This is necessary since truth is welcome wherever it is preached.[5]

Seemingly, some neoevangelicals tend to treat lightly the theological confusion of the day. Carnell attempted to remove some of the solid lines of distinction between opposite theological convictions. "A lot has happened in the past twenty-five years. With the decay of the Wellhausen hypothesis and the return to Biblical theology, the time is ripe for mutual signs of humility. The issues are not nearly as neat as either fundamentalism or modernism imagined."[6]

The same writer exhorted both liberals and conservatives to forego cultic thinking and sit down together in exploratory, authentic theological discussion.
Carnell believed the liberal should invite the orthodox
to theological discussion because theologians are
somewhat agreed now that man has a moral defect in
his will, and they have also reaffirmed the doctrine of
justification by faith.[7] It is suggested that evangelicals,
inside and outside the ecumenical movement, penetrate with their influence by introducing into it historic
Christianity. The specific areas which should be introduced are revelation, church unity and missions. This
introduction of evangelical Christianity into the liberal
ecumenical movement is intended to polarize the two
opposites of neoorthodoxy and liberalism. These are
the methods by which the neoevangelical proposes to
bring orthodoxy to bear upon the contemporary
theological scene.

Briefly summarized, the neoevangelical hopes to
emphasize points of agreement with the liberal and
neoorthodox rather than points of disagreement; he intends to recapture denominational status by cooperation with rather than separation from the old-line denominations regardless of their affiliations. He believes
it is necessary to recognize, appreciate and utilize to the
evangelicals' advantage the present return of the liberal
and neoorthodox to a so-called Biblical theology.

Embrace Creedal Christianity

By creedal Christianity is meant the form of expression which Christianity took in the historic creeds
of the church. The historic creeds or statements of belief were developed in the midst of doctrinal battles.
They were designed not to pronounce views and pro-
pose definitions where the Scripture was silent but
were designed to mark off the boundaries beyond
which orthodoxy could not go lest it delve into
heterodoxy. Some of these creeds have been passed
down to this present generation. Practically all of the

major denominations have accepted in varying degrees some creed for their doctrinal belief.

Neoevangelicals have sharply criticized fundamentalism for not connecting their convictions with the classical creeds of the church; this the new evangelicalism intends to do. "First of all, the evangelical embraces creedal Christianity—Christianity as expressed in the confessions of the church which is New Testament Christianity grounded upon the acceptance of the Bible as the Word of God, as plenarily inspired, and authoritative and infallible."[8] In contrast to fundamentalism, the new evangelicalism expects to organically relate the truths of revelation, rather than exhibit complacency with doctrines to their profounder systematic implications. The new evangelicalism looks back and observes that the reason for fundamentalism's failure to present a full-orbed and equally emphasized doctrinal system was because it divorced itself from the creedal statements of the church by separating itself from the denominations in its vigorous defense and adherence to the five fundamentals. While some in the new evangelical school of thought are severely critical of fundamentalism along these lines, others criticize fundamentalism for being highly creedal. Those in the latter category compare the lack of creedal adherence on the part of ecumenicists favoring church union to the rather inclusive incorporation of secondary doctrines into the independent's creed.

Return to Positive Preaching

Fundamentalism has been sharply criticized by the new evangelicals for engaging in excessive negative preaching. It has been accused of delving into personalities in its polemic against unbelief. The new evangelical emphasis is a shift to a positive declaration of the truth of God. He believes that an aggressive and forthright presentation of the Word will yield fruit without an emphasis upon the negative aspects of the Word. The return and rededication to positive and triumphant preaching is said to be the evangelical pulpit's great need of the hour. It is claimed that the basic doctrines of orthodoxy have been too often presented in a negative context without any application of the lessons of doctrine to life.

Overcome Minority Group Attitudes

The minority group attitudes were stated clearly by Carnell in *The Case for Orthodox Theology:* "These attitudes include a compulsive necessity to be right on every question, an excessive dedication to self-interest, and a cultic refusal to enter into the wider Christian dialogue."[9]

Apparently, the way which is prescribed for orthodoxy, and particularly the fundamentalist brand, to overcome these unpopular group attitudes is to recognize its insecurity. Insecurity comes to orthodoxy because of neglect of its own traditions. Carnell seemed to imply that the great doctrines of the faith have always been defended in history by calm and pious men without any narrow group attitudes. This is hardly the case, however, when the seven great ecumenical councils are examined more objectively. Orthodoxy is also said to be insecure because it fails to practice what it preaches. It has become cultic in allowing petty beliefs to produce such minority group attitudes.

Bear the Mark of a True Disciple

Love, not doctrine, marks off the true disciple from the false one. The new evangelicalism proposes to return to Jesus and Scripture by placing love in its proper focus. It is that which edifies while doctrine produces pride. Love, it is claimed, will cause differences even in doctrine and behavior to appear very insignificant. Carnell, who specified this solution as a part of the future for a return to classical orthodoxy, claimed a shift in emphasis had taken place from the plain injunction of Jesus to love one another to a defense of orthodox doctrine by the fundamentalist or cultic element in orthodoxy. "This shift in criteria places believers at the disposal of demonic pretense, for not only is Satan an accomplished student of Scripture, but the demons often address Jesus with language used by the angels."[10]

In somewhat sweeping and blanket statements, fundamentalists have been taken to task for failing to exhibit love. They have been accused of denouncing all who oppose them as "modernists," "liberals" or "compromisers." The neoevangelicals wish to be placed in contrast to these "ultra-fundamentalists." They hold love to be the imperative as explained by the Lord (John 13:34, 35). "For those who hold this position (sometimes termed neo-evangelical), neo-orthodox Christians are to be loved as part of the Body of Christ, just as orthodox Christians are to be loved, providing doctrinal agreement on the cardinal truths of the Christian message is reached."[11] The same writer saw two dangers in this conflict of love versus doctrine:

> First of all, doctrine alone must never become so important that in itself it becomes an end rather than a means to an end. . . . Secondly, while love for the brethren is the seal of discipleship (John 13:34-35; 1 John 3:14) and the "life of Christ" of paramount importance, if it is not accompanied by confession of sound doctrine, it is rightly adjudged a counterfeit "love and life" and must also be rejected (2 John 9-11). While it is possible to hold doctrine apart from love and the life of Christ, it is impossible to truly love the brethren and live the "life in Christ" apart from basic beliefs. Christianity is a creed as well as a way of life.[12]

". . . Love remains unsatisfied until *all* who form the body of Christ are united in one sacred fellowship."[13]

Return to the Classical View of the Church

Though Carnell is responsible for the statement of this solution, it is supported by a large majority of other

neoevangelicals. By the classical view of the church is
meant a nonseparatist view. Most defenders of the new
evangelicalism deny the doctrine of ecclesiastical separation (the separation of orthodox churches from apostate denominations). Some are even quite extreme in
ridiculing personal separation. The inconsistency of
claiming to be true to Bible doctrine and at the same
time defending a separatist view of the church stems
from the error of confusing the possession of truth with
the possession of virtue according to Carnell.[14] The
question may rightly be asked, What was the classical
view of the church on this matter? Carnell gave the
following principles to define orthodoxy's traditional
and classical view:[15]

1. All other things being equal, a Christian should
remain in the fellowship that gave him spiritual birth.
In support of this the case of Paul is cited since he did
not minister to the Gentiles until he had preached to
the Jews first. Also, Christ came unto His own, thus
providing an example.

2. A Christian should judge the claims of a church
by its official creed or confession, not by the lives of its
members. The support for this so-called traditional or
classical view is gained by implying that the separatist
issue revolves around the members who are unfaithful
or immoral. Since false priests were in the temple and
did not make it any less the house of God and the
presence of the betrayer did not make the apostles any
less a perfect instrument of God, Carnell assumed it
unwise to judge a church or denomination on the basis
of its members or leaders. As far as this neoevangelical
leader was concerned, a denomination may take active
steps to preach a false gospel and yet be a part of the
Christian Church. As long as the gospel is in print in
the denomination's creed and the members are free to
declare the gospel and protest against abuses, the denomination may be called a part of the church and
should thereby be judged.

3. Separation from an existing denomination is

justifiable on only two criteria. The two criteria which Carnell stated actually invalidate any separation at all. The two he stated are *eviction* and *apostasy*. It seems rather obvious that eviction is not the believer separating from the apostate denomination but the denomination ostracizing the believer. According to Carnell, apostasy is not present unless the denomination removes the gospel from its confession and doctrinal statement or refuses to allow the believer to preach it. This view places more emphasis upon written statements and creeds which were believed and lived long ago than upon verbal declarations and pronouncements which are believed and promoted today. Such a view disregards the fact that new meanings have been assigned to many of the historic statements of faith. All of this is understandable because Carnell did not believe in separation. "But after a few encounters with fundamentalism I realized I was not a separatist by nature, nor could I discover any Biblical warrant for the separatist position. To the contrary, all relevant evidence pointed in the other direction."[16]

This desire to return to the classical view of the church has been proposed by others with equal fervor. Neoevangelicalism expects to pursue this type of a solution. Generally speaking, they do not intend to repudiate the reformation principle but want to impress men with their responsibility to remain within their denominations unless they have officially repudiated Biblical Christianity. Various explanations have been offered of texts which the fundamentalists interpret as clearly teaching separation. Typical of the explanations is the following in reference to 2 Corinthians 6:17:

> But the coming out was a religious separation from the pagan temples. Separation is to be in the heart. It is wrong to interpret it to mean that we are to separate from a Christian denomination and it is also wrong to interpret it to mean that we are to establish Christian life as an ascetic monasticism. . . . Separation is a matter of the heart and that only.[17]

Another evidence of a desire to remain intact with the denominations is the emphasis upon the perils of independency. These are stated differently but summarized very well under three points. It tends to produce a divisive spirit. It refuses to communicate with those with whom it is in disagreement. It assumes that true independency implies individualism.[18] These are not intended to be blanket criticisms but points of danger with which the independents must wrestle. Though the new evangelicalism proposes to foster true ecumenicity by setting forth the New Testament teaching on true unity, especially in *Christianity Today*, it nevertheless recognizes the perils of ecumenicity also.[19]

Fresh and Pervading Concept of the Christian Life

Neoevangelicals expect to move beyond fundamentalism with a higher and more noble ethic. Whereas the fundamentalist stressed the matter of Christian ethics from a negative external aspect, the new evangelical approach is to probe deeper into the positive internal aspects. Instead of emphasizing the don'ts relative to Christian living, he intends to exalt the dos. The failure of fundamentalism in this area is said to be due to a minimizing of the exemplary side of Jesus' life. The nature of the fundamentalist-modernist controversy necessitated an emphasis upon the deity of Christ and thus the humanity of Christ with its perfection and ideal qualities was neglected according to the neoevangelical appraisal.

Contemporary evangelicals also want to stress more emphatically the entire moral law of God. Love toward God and neighbor is to be more fully expounded. The legalism and absoluteness so often found in fundamentalism is to be replaced with a new emphasis upon the fruit of the Spirit for dedicated Christian living. The great desire is to move beyond a definition of surrender which is related only to the self-denial of worldly practices. Surrender to God and the spiritual life involves more than externalities. Spirituality includes the invisible but real products of personality such as attitudes and motives.

The desire for a fresh and pervading concept of the Christian life is clearly revealed by Carnell's stern criticisms of the negative ethic of fundamentalism. In broad, sweeping and all-inclusive statements, he criticized individuals in the cultic element of orthodoxy (by which he means fundamentalism) of being engaged in an attempt to gain status in the cult by pleasing the cult leaders and by refraining from wrong and questionable practices.[20]

A New Concern for Individuals Which Will Result in Social Implications

Neoevangelicalism broadens its judgment at this juncture by accusing not only fundamentalism but also liberalism and neoorthodoxy for not having made a soteriological (salvation) impact upon society. The new evangelicalism hopes to recover this divine imperative and centrality of the gospel. ". . . Hope for a new society is best mediated to any nation through the spiritual regeneration of its masses."[21]

The clarion call of the new evangelicalism is for passionate participants with the existing reform movements which are set to the task of eliminating such evils as aggressive warfare, racial hatred, the liquor traffic and the exploitation of labor and management. Neoevangelicals grant that many of the contemporary reform movements are spearheaded by non-evangelicals; yet, they insist that this fact need not stifle the evangelical's interest and participation. Evangelicals are encouraged to provide proper leadership in the social reform movements. They are to constantly point out that the only adequate solution of societal problems is to be found in the redemption of Christ. When evangelicals find themselves united with liberals and humanists to bring about reform, they must express their opposition to social evils. The only occasion when an evangelical should not unite with an existing reform movement, regardless of the company he must keep, is when that group clearly rules out the option of redemption as a means to achieve its goals.

This emphasis is acknowledged by neoevangelicals as a different application of orthodox Christianity. It is an emphasis which is able to say "Christ is the answer" in such a way that He and His teachings along with all of Biblical Christianity become translated into the present society here and now. The evangelical's view of all the major doctrines of historic orthodoxy are to have their effects upon the contemporary scene. This, it is argued, is precisely what fundamentalism fails to do. It has failed in this specific because it does not recognize the relevance of the gospel to the social scene.

Some of the representatives of the new evangelicalism realize that their intended desire to change society borders on the intentions of the liberal promoters of the old social gospel. They are quick to deny, however, any vital relation. It is not infrequently admitted that the way to a new society is through the redemption of individuals and a proclamation of the gospel of Christ. These assertions are somewhat paradoxical in light of some of the other claims for a redeemed society.

A Christian University

Theological climate can always be judged by the schools which are producing the man for the pulpit. It may quite accurately be said, as the schools go so go the churches. The proposed solution of a Christian university would afford the opportunity to put into operation in a more tangible way the other solutions which have been suggested above. The university which is envisioned is not to replace nor to be superimposed upon the existing Christian schools. It is rather to go beyond the existing evangelical educational facilities. It is to be supradenominational. Obviously, such an institution would not be able to commit itself to any denominational creed or belief. Probably it could not ask any ınore of its faculty members than that they give honest assent to the articles of the Apostles' Creed. This university is to be of the highest academic excellence, demanding above all else intellectual freedom.

Neoevangelicals see the need for such a Christian university arising from several areas: the evangelical penetration of American Christianity has turned away many young people in search for Christ-centered collegiate studies; the missionary cause demands workers who are not only trained in the Bible but also the secular fields; there is a need for teachers and leaders to uphold and defend our faith and freedom; and no existing interdenominational institution compares in reputation with the familiar and well-known secular universities of our day.

This Christian university, it is contended, must be staffed by those who have a deep sense of personal devotion to the Lord. The school must deal with its subject matter, which is to be rather inclusive, in the rich context of the Bible. The faculty members are to engage in research and writing rather than preaching and promotional activities.[22] It is hoped that this venture, which is arousing considerable interest, will promote the desired intellectuality of the new evangelicalism, help break down denominational barriers which are destructive of church unity, and retrieve Christian scholarship which fundamentalism neglected at the cost of preaching.

Any unbiased fundamentalist will admit that some of the above solutions present valid means of accomplishing, at least in part, the task of the church. There are notable elements in most of them. It is certainly well to disown the modernist perversion of Biblical theology. There is a great need for a positive preaching of the eternal truth of God. Petty differences ought not divide the Body of Christ. Who would argue that love is not to be characteristic of the true disciple? Certainly, the gospel must be brought to bear upon the society in which we live. The desire for a new concept of the Christian life with its liberties and limitations is always welcome. Obviously, God does not place a premium on ignorance, and the servant of God needs to be trained in the most adequate fashion. God's work deserves the best in every area.

The weaknesses of these solutions should also be understood if an objective and adequate appraisal is to be made. In rejecting the so-called fundamentalist "reduction" of Biblical theology, one fears the very real danger of rejecting the fundamentalist "religion" as well. Positive preaching is necessary, but it is hermeneutically unsound and theologically unwise to interpret a negative scriptural statement only by stating its positive implications. It is equally as unsound and unwise to interpret a positive scriptural statement only by stating its negative implications. Minority group attitudes ought not divide and should be overcome; but it must be borne in mind that majority group attitudes may also divide and can be wrong and, therefore, should also be overcome. Love as a mark of a true disciple cannot be determined by the gauge of agreement. In the neoevangelical emphasis upon love rather than doctrine it is easy to forget that love itself is also a doctrine. The drastic need of the hour is for the gospel to be made applicable to our world; yet, the danger of watering down the gospel in order to make it acceptable to the world and altering to society is very real. Legality must never replace the liberty which is the believer's in Christ, but it is equally Biblical that liberty must not degenerate into license. Intellectualism, properly balanced with spirituality, is sorely needed. God spare the servant of the Lord, however, from a carnal desire to be intellectual only for the sake of intellectuality. It is a means to an end, and the means must not be worshiped. The ideal of a supradenominational Christian university may have its advantages in a pursuit of intellectual freedom. Yet, this would tend to do away with denominational distinctions which are also a part of intellectual freedom.

The present status of the new evangelicalism can be summarized under the three methods by which the foregoing proposed solutions are being accomplished—penetration, education and Christianization.

Through the National Association of Evangelicals on the national scene and the World Evangelical Fellowship on the international scene, the new evangelicalism is being represented. Through these organizations the neoevangelical is seeking to have his message penetrate into the world and to provide an opportunity to make evangelicalism respectable to the liberal and neoorthodox.

The emphasis upon education is evident in the desire for a Christian university and for existing theological seminaries to seek the approval of the American Association of Theological Seminaries. Also, men of the neoevangelical persuasion are producing a flood of new literature from the best publishers.

The societal impact which neoevangelicalism proposes to make fosters the connotation of a *Christianization* of society. Neoevangelicals do not deny that there is but one gospel and that it is an individual gospel. Their emphasis, however, sometimes savors of the hope of a redeemed society. Mass evangelism on the international and national scene also lends support to this connotation.

NOTES

1. Henry, *Evangelical Responsibility*, p. 48.
2. Ockenga, "The New Evangelicalism," pp. 4, 5.
3. Harold J. Ockenga, "Resurgent Evangelical Leadership," *Christianity Today* (October 10, 1960), p. 12.
4. Ibid.
5. Blaiklock, "Conservatism," p. 33.
6. Carnell, "Orthodoxy," p. 378.
7. Ibid., pp. 377, 378.
8. Ockenga, "The New Evangelicalism," p. 6.
9. Carnell, *The Case for Orthodox Theology*, p. 127.
10. Ibid., p. 128.

11. Walter R. Martin, "Love, Doctrine and Fellowship," *Eternity* (November 1960), p. 22.

12. Ibid., pp. 55, 56.

13. Carnell, *The Case for Orthodox Theology*, p. 137.

14. Ibid., p. 132.

15. Ibid., pp. 133-137.

16. Carnell, "Orthodoxy," p. 378.

17. Donald G. Barnhouse, "Hollywood and Christian Separation," *Eternity* (June 1960), p. 5.

18. "The Perils of Independency," *Christianity Today* (November 12, 1956).

19. For the proposed ministry of *Christianity Today*, see the October 15, 1956 issue. For "The Perils of Ecumenicity," see the November 26, 1956 issue.

20. Carnell, *The Case for Orthodox Theology*, pp. 120, 121.

21. "Where Do We Go from Here?" *Christianity Today* (November 12, 1956), p. 18.

22. "Why a Christian University?" *Christianity Today* (October 10, 1960), pp. 24, 25; "Do We Need a Christian University?" *Christianity Today* (May 9, 1960), pp. 3-6.

Varieties and Basic Tenets of Neoevangelicalism

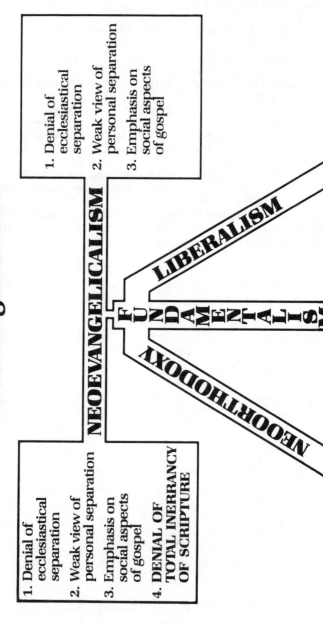

NEOEVANGELICALISM

1. Denial of ecclesiastical separation
2. Weak view of personal separation
3. Emphasis on social aspects of gospel

1. Denial of ecclesiastical separation
2. Weak view of personal separation
3. Emphasis on social aspects of gospel
4. DENIAL OF TOTAL INERRANCY OF SCRIPTURE

LIBERALISM

FUNDAMENTALISM

NEOORTHODOXY

Part II

DOCTRINES

1

Scripture

IT IS BECOMING increasingly more evident that the issue which divides the neoevangelical from the evangelical or fundamentalist is not the dance, smoking, card playing or movies. It is Biblical authority. Matters of personal separation and "failures" in the application of the gospel to society have become the scapegoats used by neoevangelicalism to hide a far more serious disagreement which it has with fundamentalism. While some neoevangelicals candidly subscribe to the total inerrancy of Scripture, others—and the number is steadily increasing—either refuse to commit themselves, subordinate Scripture to other considerations, or subscribe to viewpoints which make belief in total inerrancy completely untenable. Some neoevangelicals are willing to make concessions relative to the historical validity of the creation accounts in Genesis, Adam and Eve as historic personages, the universality of the flood and even verbal inspiration of Scripture.

The weak views of Scripture here presented represent a significant and dangerous trend in the new evangelical camp. These views are not shared by all, but they are shared by too many.

The doctrine of Scripture has been often and ably presented. The historical development of the doctrines of revelation, inspiration and authority are squarely on the side of conservatism and need not be argued here. Through an accurate definition of the term *doctrine* as opposed to the term *dogma* and by reviewing the history of the doctrine it can be established that "in the cases of revelation and inspiration a continuous, consistent, and practically unanimous doctrine essentially identical with the conservative doctrine of the present existed until almost 1800."[1]

It is always valuable to consider the beliefs of the church from its beginning. However, the Bible must be the final court of appeal whether its teachings have been promoted in the church or not. That the Bible contains material for the formulation of a doctrine of Scripture may be proven from the teachings of Christ. The Bible doctrine is also based upon the testimony of other portions of Scripture. The classic passages presenting the Bible doctrine are 2 Timothy 3:16; 2 Peter 1:20, 21; John 10:34, 35 and Matthew 5:17, 18.[2]

Some neoevangelicals have questioned the dogmatic statements of those who hold to the doctrine of verbal plenary inspiration and thus the complete inerrancy of Scripture. The first public request for a reinvestigation of this view came in 1956 and was published in *Christian Life*.[3] Paul King Jewett expressed a similar desire. He wrote: ". . . Our all important Protestant conviction of Biblical authority needs revitalizing."[4] The areas which Jewett listed as those needing revitalization were Scripture translation, Biblical authority and the doctrine of scriptural inspiration. He desired this reinvestigation in accordance with helpful Biblical criticism.

Carnell, whose views were not always shared by his brethren, stated his neoevangelical position dogmatically:

> Contemporary orthodoxy does very little to sustain the classical dialogue on inspiration. The

fountain of new ideas has apparently run dry, for what was once a live issue in the church has now ossified into a theological tradition. As a result a heavy pall of fear hangs over the academic community. When a gifted professor tries to interact with the critical difficulties in the text, he is charged with disaffection, if not outright heresy. Orthodoxy forgets one important verdict of history: namely, that when truth is presented in a poor light, tomorrow's leaders may embrace error on the single reason that it is more persuasively defended.[5]

The same writer expressed his own problem by attributing it to the whole of orthodoxy when he said, "The problem of inspiration is *still* a problem."[6]

The book by Ramm, *Special Revelation and the Word of God*, has much to commend it; yet the writer reveals a dissatisfaction with the fundamentalist doctrine of Scripture. Walvoord, in his review of the book, pointed this out: "Dr. Ramm feels that fundamentalism is guilty of incipient bibliolatry and that neo-orthodoxy is deficient in its concept of revelation as simply 'an encounter,' because revelation is 'both a knowing and an experience of the living God' (p. 7)."[7]

Ronald H. Nash stated his dissatisfaction with the fundamentalist doctrine of Scripture very plainly: "Whether it be for good or ill, evangelicals are willing to reopen the subject of the inspiration of the Scriptures."[8]

From a careful study of neoevangelical literature, it appears that there are several reasons for the above interest in the reinvestigation of the doctrine of Scripture. Probably the basic reason which has led to the reopening of the doctrine has been the neoevangelical desire to present an intellectually acceptable position to those with whom the neoevangelical desires to meet in theological table talk. Walton stated this fact well:

> This emphasis on scholarship appears to be basic to the New Evangelical movement. Concessions are made to science in the name of scholarly opin-

ion. The doctrine of Biblical inspiration is re-opened because of the influence of liberalism, especially neo-orthodoxy. Inspiration is further re-evaluated because of the problems that have been introduced by rationalistic textual criticism. Ideas are exchanged with Liberal theologians because of an unwillingness to share the "intellectual stagnation" that men like Carnell attribute to Fundamentalism.[9]

Ockenga voiced this very desire on the part of neoevangelicalism when he said that the neoevangelical "desires to win a new respectability for orthodoxy in the academic circles by producing scholars who can defend the faith on intellectual ground."[10]

Carnell's book, *The Case for Orthodox Theology*, is given over to a large extent to the downgrading of the fundamentalist intellectualism.[11]

These repentant fundamentalists express a dangerous subservience to science. The desire to gain intellectual acceptability has led to a friendly attitude toward science almost to the point of placing scholarship and science in the seat of authority. The threshold evolution of Edward John Carnell and the progressive creationism of Bernard Ramm are clear evidences of semantic delusions and needless concessions of the Word of God to science.

Many evidences of this trend reveal a reason for dissatisfaction, but only a few need to be cited here. Ockenga said in an Associated Press dispatch from Boston on December 8, 1957:

> The evangelical believes that Christianity is intellectually defensible, that the Christian cannot be obscurantist in scientific questions pertaining to the creation, the age of man, the universality of the flood and other debatable Biblical questions. . . . The new evangelicalism is willing to face the intellectual problems and meet them in the framework of modern learning.[12]

Barnhouse expressed serious doubt of the validity of the historic orthodox interpretation of the first chap-

ters of Genesis in his article, "Adam and Modern Sci-   77
ence." Speaking of the attitude which the Christian   •
ought to take toward evolution, which Barnhouse
called a model, he said:

> The fact is (and there is no harm to confess it), that
> we Christians do not have a model that will syn-
> thetize the findings in nature and the statements
> of Scripture. And until we do, we have to be care-
> ful about pulling down the scientific model that is
> functioning so well in all the laboratories of the
> world. We do not have a better one. We live in
> hope that a better one will be forthcoming, but it
> has not yet been advanced.[13]

Bernard Ramm deals extensively with the relation
of science and the inerrancy of Scripture and leaves the
impression that Scripture ought to be interpreted in the
light of science.[14] In another work the same writer
voiced an attitude which causes deep concern:

> If the differences between the sciences and the
> Bible were to grow to a very large number and
> were of the most serious nature, it would be ques-
> tionable if we could retain faith in Scripture. True,
> we may believe *some* of the Bible 'in spite of' sci-
> ence, but certainly the situation would change if
> we believe *all* of the Bible in spite of science.[15]

Carnell displayed his willingness to interpret the
Bible in the light of science when he said:

> The Genesis account implies an act of immediate
> creation, but the same account also implies that
> God made the world in six literal days; and since
> orthodoxy has given up the literal-day theory out
> of respect for geology, it would certainly forfeit no
> principle if it gave up the immediate-creation
> theory out of respect for paleontology. The two
> seem to be quite parallel.[16]

Certainly Sanderson was right when he said,
"Neo-Evangelicalism's 'friendly attitude toward science' has gone hand in hand with the 'reopening of the
subject of Biblical inspiration.'"[17]

Some deviations have already been presented in

the above discussion of the dissatisfactions which neoevangelicals have with the doctrine of Scripture. Other deviations are clearly evident in the neoevangelical approach.

This does not mean that the doctrine of Scripture does not receive consideration in neoevangelicalism. It does mean that in relation to the soteriological and societal emphasis in neoevangelicalism, Bibliology becomes a secondary issue. The importance of the Bible and yet its second place in relation to soteriology is clearly implied by Eldersveld.[18] The neoevangelical feels that one's view of the Bible should be in line with consistent modern discoveries. Ketcham accurately observed that the shifting of emphasis from Biblical authority to soteriology means that the neoevangelical has shifted the emphasis "from the authority of Bible doctrine to the realm of human experience."[19]

Ockenga and Carnell both stressed the necessity of connecting convictions with the classical creeds of the church. They did so to the extent that one gets the impression that creedal Christianity has always been Biblical Christianity, which is not the case. Ockenga said, "First of all, the evangelical embraces creedal Christianity—Christianity as expressed in the confessions of the church. . . ."[20] Carnell claimed that "fundamentalists failed to connect their convictions with the classical creeds of the church."[21] He stated elsewhere, "Orthodoxy is insecure because it neglects the majesty of its own traditions."[22] This type of attitude indicates a desire to place authority in the church and the creeds.

Another sign of weakness is the growing tendency to give the words of Christ and gospel passages a special place of priority over the rest of the Word of God. Carnell implied this was his position when he said: *"Since Jesus received his doctrine from the Father, everything that Jesus says is true on divine authority.* Any other position leads to skepticism."[23] One would wish Carnell and others would agree with the Savior's view of the total inerrancy of Scripture.

Carnell demonstrates how far one neoevangelical is willing to go in order to make a case for orthodoxy before the liberal and neoorthodox. Take as an example such a questionable statement as this: "The lower stages have to be read in the light of the higher, with the correction which the higher affords."[24] Carnell's criticism of Calvinism as cultic since it seldom appreciates the extent to which the New Testament ethic judges the truncated ethic of the Old Testament revealed clearly his desire to place more authority on some portions of the Bible than on others. The most obvious differentiation of the authority of Scripture came when he practically discounted doctrine that is not clearly set forth in either Romans or Galatians.[25]

This fact has been noted by critics of the new evangelicalism for some time but was brought out clearly in a survey sponsored by *Christianity Today*. The most alarming admission of the report was that the issue which distinguished the fundamentalist clergy from the conservative was the doctrine of Scripture. Fundamentalists subscribed to total or complete inerrancy, whereas those who were considered conservatives either did not subscribe to total inerrancy or had doubts about the doctrine.[26]

DeWolf, a neoliberal and thus one whom neoevangelicals hope to win by their concessions, observed the revision of the doctrine of inspiration in neoevangelical theology. He wrote:

> There is a noticeable, though indecisive change in the doctrine of biblical inspiration and authority. Some of the new evangelicals, unlike most of the fundamentalists, avoid teaching "verbal" inspiration of the Bible, stressing rather plenary or full inspiration. This marks a movement to a more flexible position.[27]

There is a growing hesitancy on the part of many neoevangelicals to accept the *verbal* inspiration of Scripture. Neoevangelicalism cannot deny this because the word *verbal* is conspicuous by its absence in their discussions of inspiration. When writing of an inspired Bible, neoevangelicals often use the term *plenary inspiration* instead of *verbal plenary inspiration.*

Walvoord sees evidence of a conceptual theory of inspiration as opposed to a verbal plenary theory in Ramm's book, *Special Revelation and the Word of God.* He wrote:

> While clearly on the side of conservative orthodoxy, his treatment seems to embrace a dynamic or conceptual theory of inspiration as illustrated in the following sentence: "Because the same thought (or meaning) can be expressed by different words the relationship is *dynamic* or *flexible* and not *fixed* or *mechanical*" (p. 178).[28]

Agreeing with the neoevangelical viewpoint, Warren C. Young said: "Any type of verbal inspiration which fails to recognize the conceptual side will not carry much weight today."[29]

Dewey M. Beegle, who, according to Charles C. Ryrie, has given expression to the Biblical viewpoint of some neoevangelicals,[30] not only expressed hesitancy to accept verbal inspiration but flatly denied it. "We need to remind ourselves that the verbal plenary formulation of inspiration is, after all, only a doctrine—a non-Biblical doctrine at that."[31]

These quotations should illustrate that neoevangelicalism hesitates to accept verbal inspiration of the Scriptures. A notable exception to this was expressed by Carl F. H. Henry. In a lively critique of *The Inspiration of Scripture* by Dewey M. Beegle, Henry stated clearly his acceptance of the verbal inerrancy of Scripture: "The Scriptures assert that inspiration extended not only to chosen persons but to their sacred writings, and that the very words derive their unique authority from this supernatural superintendence."[32]

While Henry's public admission of verbal inspiration and inerrancy is welcome, one reads with mixed emotions his statement about the view of inerrancy held by the Biblical writers in the same review. He wrote: "Evangelical theologians acknowledge that inerrancy is not formally claimed by the biblical writers. But they assert that it is a proper inference from the Bible's teaching about its own inspiration, and from the character of the self-revealing God."[33]

Similar words of hesitancy come from the pen of Everett F. Harrison:

> Unquestionably the Bible teaches its own inspiration. It is the Book of God. *It does not require us to hold inerrancy* [italics not in original], *though this is a natural corollary of full inspiration.* The phenomena which present difficulties are not to be dismissed or underrated. They have driven many sincere believers in the trustworthiness of the Bible as a spiritual guide to hold a modified position on the non-revelation material. Every man must be persuaded in his own mind.[34]

Here is expressed hesitancy to accept total inerrancy in all the Bible—revelational and nonrevelational. Also, Harrison places the responsibility of determining the Bible's view of its own inerrancy at the mercy of man's mind.

Edward John Carnell confessed his own problem in relation to proposed theological and historical errors in Scripture in his conversation with Karl Barth in Chicago. Carnell's question to Barth was, " 'How does Dr. Barth harmonize his appeal to Scripture as the objective Word of God with his admission that Scripture is sullied by errors, theological as well as historical or factual?' Carnell confessed parenthetically that 'this is a problem for me, too.' "[35]

An attempt to modify Carnell's position and poor testimony before Barth appeared in *Christianity Today*. The article implied that the author of the first article was left with the impression that Carnell did not believe in an inerrant Scripture. Incidentally, Clark is not alone in that impression. In the same article, Carnell's statement of his view of Scripture to the Fuller Seminary chapel was given. After admitting his problems Carnell said: ". . . I now believe and always have be-

lieved plenary inspiration of Scripture."[36] This statement does not free Carnell from the charge of failing to
believe in verbal inspiration and total inerrancy of
Scripture, even nonrevealed matters, because it is lacking in two great esentials. It is lacking by the omission
of the word *verbal* and the word *complete* inerrancy of
Scripture.

The tendency to distinguish between inspiration
and inerrancy is obvious in Nash's work. He evidently
prefers the term "adequacy" to "inerrancy." He con-
veniently evaded the issue of inerrancy by cluttering it
with matters of translation difficulties. "The autographs may have been *inerrant* while later translations
and versions are adequate, albeit not perfect, repre-
sentations of the original message."[37] He further
stated, "Contemporary evangelicals are pointing out
that inspiration and inerrancy are not equivalent con-
cepts."[38] And again, "Strictly speaking, the Bible does
not teach the inerrancy of its original manuscripts."[39]

With special reference to the words of Harrison
cited above but with general reference to all who express this distinction between inspiration and inerrancy, Ryrie stated:

> In other words, some, because of apparent dif-
> ficulties in the Bible (such as historical and
> chronological problems) are concluding that these
> sections are not inerrant though inspired. One
> hears more and more these days: "I believe the
> Bible is inspired, but I cannot believe that it is
> without error." Inspiration, yes; verbal inspira-
> tion, no. Why is it so? One cannot see motives,
> but for some it is the result of honest wrestling
> with problems which have shaken their faith. For
> others, one cannot help but feel that it is part of
> the current worship of intellectualism as a sacred
> cow and a necessary step in achieving the appro-
> bation of godless intellectuals so-called."[40]

This tendency to distinguish between inspiration
and complete inerrancy has been called the "double-
revelation theory" by John C. Whitcomb.[41] In his cri-

> Briefly stated, this theory maintains that God has given to man two revelations of truth, each of which is fully authoritative in its own realm: the revelation of God in Scriptures and the revelation of God in nature. . . . The theologian is the God-appointed interpreter of Scripture and the scientist is the God-appointed interpreter of nature, and each has specialized tools for determining the true meaning of the particular book of revelation which he is called upon to study.[42]

This type of approach to Scripture which is being advocated by neoevangelical scholars allows them to apply inspiration and inerrancy only to matters of faith and life in the Scriptures and not to peripheral matters. Peripheral matters would include whatever the individual decides is not a matter of faith and life, such as problems of the origin of the universe, the solar system, the earth, man, the magnitude and effects of the flood, minor historical details, grammatical constructions, etc.

Beegle's extreme viewpoint regarding Scripture is the end product of the neoevangelical desire to accommodate the Bible to science. He wrote: "The inductive evidence of the New Testament indicates that Jesus taught a strong doctrine of inspiration and authority of Scripture, yet without claiming inerrancy."[43] Again he said: "But minor historical errors in Scripture invalidate neither our faith nor true doctrine."[44]

Joseph A. Hill, in a report of George Stob's view of infallibility presented as a lecture at Trinity College, clearly distinguished the neoevangelical view of inspiration and the traditional orthodox position set forth by Warfield and by Edward J. Young in *Thy Word Is Truth*. Hill wrote:

> There are in the present controversy two theories as to the nature of inspiration. These are as follows: 1. Inspiration makes certain that we have an authoritative record of all that God wanted to make known. But it was not God's intention or purpose to secure inerrancy in peripheral matters.

'Peripheral matters' include Scriptural data which have nothing to do with faith and life, such as minor historical details, grammatical constructions, and the like. 2. The other view is that inspiration applies to all the data of Scripture, including peripheral matters. Every word of the Bible, all grammatical points and every historical detail, however trivial, are God-breathed. According to this view the Bible is free from all error, discrepancy, and inaccuracy.[45]

Daniel P. Fuller, in a guest paper read at the annual meeting of the Evangelical Theological Society in Toronto December 27, 1967, gave expression to the first theory as to the nature of inspiration expressed above. The weak view of Scripture held by men such as Fuller has caused a rift within the new evangelical school of thought. The issue is simply, Is the Bible inerrant in all its pronouncements, or is it merely an inerrant record of some inspired truth? The gulf between neoevangelicalism has been widening over the matter of the inerrancy of Scripture. Strong expressions of dissatisfaction with belief in anything less than the total inerrancy of Scripture have appeared in the *Bulletin of the Evangelical Theological Society*.[46]

However much the neoevangelical may seek refuge for his view of Scripture in the views of Scripture held by James Orr, Matthew Henry and others, he is still in blatant contradiction with the view of Scripture held by Christ. One's view of Scripture must not be derived or defended merely from the views of others, however high a regard for Scripture they may or may not have had. The conservative must find his view of Scripture from the Scriptures.

The subjectivity in the neoevangelical view may not be as decided as in the neoorthodox and neoliberal views, but it is there nonetheless.

Harold Lindsell, former editor of *Christianity Today*, commented on the presence of some among the new evangelicals who no longer believe in an inerrant Scripture. "Today there are those who have been numbered among the new evangelicals, some of whom possess the keenest minds, and have acquired the apparati of scholarship, who have broken or are in the process of breaking with the doctrine of an inerrant Scripture."[47] The same writer donned the role of a prophet as he predicted a dangerous future for those who will hold such a weak view of Scripture and consequently for the church as well. One must fearfully agree with his prediction:

> . . . One can predict with almost fatalistic certainty that, in due course of time, the moderating evangelicals who deny inerrancy will adopt new positions, such as belief in the multiple authorship of Isaiah, the late date of Daniel, the idea that the first eleven chapters of Genesis are myth and saga, and then these critical conclusions will spill over into the New Testament, and when the same principles of higher criticisms are applied, this can only lead to a scrapping of the facticity of the resurrection, etc. This has ever been the historical movement and there is nothing to suppose that such a repetitive process will not follow.[48]

Whatever the motives may be and however high a view of Scripture the neoevangelical may claim to espouse, the deviations cited above represent serious differences with the view of Scripture presented by Christ and the human penmen of Holy Scripture. These differences are dangerous. If carried to their logical conclusions, they may well evaporate the need for any special revelation from God. If God may not be trusted in the things He has revealed which do not relate to faith and life, how may He be trusted at all? How is one to decide what is a matter of faith and life and what is not?

The Lord's teaching regarding the abiding character of the very words of Scripture—including the letters and parts of letters making up the words (Matt. 5:17-19)—presents His teaching of complete verbal inerrancy if it presents anything at all. Also, Christ's emphasis upon the impossibility of annulling or breaking the words of Scripture is absolutely meaningless if He did not teach verbal plenary inspiration and thus complete inerrancy both in that which was revealed directly by God and that which might be classified as nonrevelational material (John 10:33-36). The Lord went so far as to teach the inerrancy not only of words, but He extended it to the grammatical form of the verb (Matt. 22:32).

Christ made no distinction between facts of history, geography, science or theology. He referred to them all—to that which was directly revealed by God and to that which was not so revealed—always endorsing the Scriptures with the divine authority which they possessed and investing them with His own divine authority (Matt. 5:17, 18; Luke 24:44; John 10:34, 35).

Thus, Christ is not completely nor accurately preached unless His view of Scripture be accepted in spite of problems which the human mind may encounter. There were problems of translation and distance from the originals when Christ spoke; yet this did not keep Him from accepting the Scriptures in their entirety as the verbally inerrant Word of God.

NOTES

1. John A. Witmer, "A Critical Study of Current Trends in Bibliology" (Th.D. dissertation, Dallas Theological Seminary, 1953), p. 89.

2. For an excellent discussion of these and others, see Benjamin B. Warfield, *The Inspiration and Authority of the Bible* (Philadelphia: Presbyterian Reformed Publishing Co., 1948), pp. 131-168. The attacks on these and other central texts by Dewey M. Beegle and Daniel B. Stevick have only further proven the subjective nature of unbelieving opposition.

3. "Is Evangelical Theology Changing?" *Christian Life* (March 1956), p. 17.

4. Paul King Jewett, "Biblical Authority, a Crucial Issue in Protestantism," *United Evangelical Action* (May 1, 1953), p. 9.

5. Carnell, *The Case for Orthodox Theology,* p. 110.

6. Ibid., p. 109.

7. John F. Walvoord, review of *Special Revelation and the Word of God* by Bernard Ramm, *Bibliotheca Sacra* (October 1961), p. 347.

8. Ronald H. Nash, *The New Evangelicalism* (Grand Rapids: Zondervan Publishing House, 1963), p. 35.

9. Dennis M. Walton, "An Identification of New Evangelicalism" (B.D. thesis, Central Conservative Baptist Theological Seminary, 1961), pp. 55, 56.

10. Ockenga, "Resurgent Evangelical Leadership," p. 14.

11. Carnell, *The Case for Orthodox Theology*, pp. 120ff.

12. Harold J. Ockenga, "The New Evangelicalism," *Christian Beacon* (January 9, 1958), p. 1.

13. Donald G. Barnhouse, "Adam and Modern Science," *Eternity* (May 1960), p. 6.

14. Bernard Ramm, *Protestant Biblical Interpretation* (Boston: W. A. Wilde Co., 1956), pp. 182ff.

15. Bernard Ramm, *The Christian View of Science and Scripture* (Grand Rapids: Wm. B. Eerdmans Publishing Co., 1955), p. 29.

16. Carnell, *The Case for Orthodox Theology*, p. 95.

17. John W. Sanderson, "Fundamentalism and Its Critics," *The Sunday School Times* (January 21, 1961), p. 12.

18. Peter H. Eldersveld, "The Word for This World," *Christianity Today* (Januray 21, 1957), pp. 13, 14.

19. Robert T. Ketcham, "A New Peril in Our Last Days," *Christian Beacon* (May 17, 1956), p. 6.

20. Ockenga, "Resurgent Evangelical Leadership," p. 6.

21. Carnell, *The Case for Orthodox Theology*, p. 113.

22. Ibid., p. 127.

23. Ibid., p. 40.

24. Ibid., pp. 52, 53.

25. Ibid., pp. 58, 59, 66.

26. "Theological Beliefs of American Clergymen," *Christianity Today* (November 10, 1961), p. 11.

27. L. Harold DeWolf, *Present Trends in Christian Thought* (New York: Association Press, 1960), p. 40.

28. Walvoord, review of *Special Revelation and the Word of God*, p. 347.

29. Alva J. McClain, "Is Theology Changing in the Conservative Camp?" *The Brethren Missionary Herald* (February 23, 1957), p. 19.

30. Charles C. Ryrie, review of *The Inspiration of Scripture* by Dewey M. Beegle, *Bibliotheca Sacra* (January—March 1964), p. 68.

31. Dewey M. Beegle, *The Inspiration of Scripture* (Philadelphia: The Westminster Press, 1963), p. 187.

32. Carl F. H. Henry, "Yea, Hath God Said. . . ?" *Christianity Today* (April 26, 1963), p. 47.

33. Ibid., p. 26.

34. Everett F. Harrison, "The Phenomena of Scripture," *Revelation and the Bible* (Grand Rapids: Baker Book House, 1958), p. 250.

35. "Special Report: Encountering Barth in Chicago," *Christianity Today* (May 11, 1962), p. 36.

36. "Carnell on Scripture," *Christianity Today* (June 8, 1967), p. 20.

37. Nash, *The New Evangelicalism*, p. 66.

38. Ibid., p. 75.

39. Ibid., p. 76.

40. Charles C. Ryrie, "The Importance of Inerrancy," *Bibliotheca Sacra* (April—June 1963), p. 140.

41. John C. Whitcomb, "Biblical Inerrancy and the Double Revelation Theory," *Grace Journal* (Winter 1963), pp. 3-20.

42. Ibid., p. 4.

43. Beegle, *The Inspiration of Scripture*, p. 170.

44. Ibid.

45. Joseph A. Hill, "Dr. George Stob on Infallibility," *Torch and Trumpet* (January 1960), p. 6.

46. Ralph Earle, "Further Thoughts on Biblical Inspiration" (Winter 1963); Gordon R. Lewis, "What Does Biblical Infallibility Mean" (Winter 1963); Harold Lindsell, "A Historian Looks at Inerrancy" (Winter 1965); John Warwick Montgomery, "Inspiration and Inerrancy: A New Departure" (Spring 1965); "Biblical Inerrancy Today" (a report of a panel discussion moderated by John F. Walvoord, Winter 1966); J. Barton Payne, "Apeitheo: Current Resistance to Biblical Inerrancy" (Winter 1967); *Bulletin of The Evangelical Theological Society*.

47. Harold Lindsell, "A Historian Looks at Inerrancy," *Bulletin of the Evangelical Theological Society* (Winter 1965).

48. Ibid., p. 11.

2

Salvation

WITHOUT QUESTION, both in expression of belief and in practice, the doctrine which is stressed most by the new evangelicalism is the doctrine of salvation. This doctrine with its individual and societal aspects seems to be to neoevangelicals what the heart is to the human body. It is the vibrant, pulsating and life-giving center of the movement. Soteriology is the doctrine to which all others become subservient. This subserviency of other doctrines to the doctrine of salvation is revealed by the emphasis placed upon it and the lack of equal emphasis upon other important doctrines. Perhaps the neoevangelical is guilty, at this point, of committing the sin which he ascribes to the fundamentalist—the sin of trying to avoid one extreme by going to the other. Neoevangelicals have accused the fundamentalists of not making a social impact through the gospel because of their desire to preserve that gospel from the attacks of liberalism. Is it not equally feasible that neo-evangelicalism, in an attempt to emphasize the social implications of the gospel, has emphasized these to the neglect of other doctrines? Has new evangelicalism put soteriology in the place of the five fundamentals?

Humanitarianism is one of the stated emphases of the new evangelicalism. This humanitarian concern is an honest desire to have the gospel of Christ touch the social ills of man, not only on the local community level but also on the national and world scenes. The only place to which the world can turn for a true and workable solution for its vexing social problems is to the church. Most neoevangelicals very carefully stress the need for an individual response to the gospel before it can have an effect upon society. Individual response to the claims of Christ is not neglected. No element of works is injected as a substitute or aid for faith in the neoevangelical doctrine. The point of emphasis is the societal impact which this individual salvation is to have upon others.

It is no secret that our contemporary society does not show respect for the interpretation which the church gives to the world's social crises; neither does it accept or respect the guidance which the church gives in relation to the world's societal evils. The neoevangelical feels that the church in general and fundamentalism in particular are somewhat responsible for this lack of respect on the part of society. Fundamentalism fostered a socially indifferent attitude and a social pessimism as a result of its strenuous reaction to the liberal social gospel. "Its revolt against the social gospel deflected evangelical Protestantism from the spiritual vision of a Christian culture to an attitude of social 'isolationism.' "[1]

Within the neoevangelical movement there is a recognition that not only has fundamentalism failed to meet the social evils, but so has neoorthodoxy and liberalism with its now defunct social gospel message. Though both conservatives and nonconservatives failed, the reasons for their failures are different. The one failed because of a misplaced emphasis and lack of vision, while the other failed because of lack of power and supernaturalness. Nevertheless, they both failed; and the neoevangelical's desire is to utilize the good in these extremes and strike a proper balance between the doctrine of the fundamentalist and the program of the liberal. Neoevangelicals recognize that there is not a personal and a social gospel but only one gospel. "Now we know what we should have immediately recognized then, that there is only one Gospel, but that it includes both sides. . . . There is no such thing as a social gospel; conversely, there is no such thing as an asocial Christian."[2]

Concern for the crying needs of society was taught by Christ through His life and ministry. He helped those sick in body as well as those sick in soul. His concern for those who were socially maladjusted continued through His entire earthly ministry. The believer is challenged by the neoevangelical to follow the example of Christ. No Christian lives in isolation but must move from the position of spectator to participant. The individual who claims to be a follower of Christ must ask himself these questions: Am I a part of the problems which face the world, or am I part of the answer? Am I an asset or a liability to the cause of Christ? The new life which the believer has experienced ought to make itself felt upon society. The Christian is not to be of the world, but he certainly is *in* the world and, therefore, is responsible to God for his influence *upon* it. As far as the neoevangelicals are concerned, fundamentalism has failed too often in these respects. Like the priest and the Levite in the Bible, fundamentalism has bypassed suffering humanity.

In opposition to the fundamentalist's indirect influence, which came only as individuals contributed to the solving of social ills, the neoevangelical claims to be having a direct influence on the social scene. Frequently, neoevangelicals speak of a "Christian culture," a "new society" and a "new social order." It is usually made quite clear, however, that the primary task of the church is to win individuals to Christ. Henry made it clear that there is no such thing as a corporate salvation.

> How can a new social order be built without new men? How shall there be new men unless they are born again? How shall they be born again until they come to a personal and saving relationship with the Lord Jesus Christ? How shall they come to such a relationship unless they hear the Gospel?[3]

There are several methods by which the neoevangelical expects to apply the gospel to the social scene. One of these is through *Christianity Today*, the official organ of the movement.

> The appearance of the fortnightly magazine, *Christianity Today*, marked a new contemporary juncture of evangelical forces with the Reformation emphasis on Christianity as a world-life view and with the insistence on nineteenth-century American revivalism on the social significance of the Gospel.[4]

Another method which the neoevangelical suggests for the application of the gospel to global evils is for the evangelical to align himself and his church with the existing social reform movements. Any community or national effort to wage war against racial hatred, the liquor traffic, unfairness in labor and management and similar sins should have the active and positive cooperation of evangelical Christianity.

Then, too, every evangelical pastor should inveigh against social evils and injustices, not only as they relate to individuals but as they appear on the broad social scene as well. The collapse of the utopian-world idea and the failure of neoorthodoxy in this connection provide a favorable opportunity for evangelicalism to recapture leadership in pressing for a new world social order.[5] Through these three media—the press, alignment with existing social reform movements, and the pulpit—neoevangelicalism is attempting to implement a program whereby the gospel message will affect society.

An objective study of all the available material favorable to the new evangelicalism will demonstrate that salvation and the societal influence are not the only areas with which neoevangelicalism deals. Scholarly attempts have been made to defend and present the authority of the Bible. Neoevangelicals have presented a scriptural view of the Person and work of Christ. In fact, whenever any doctrine is treated, it is usually done with clarity and completeness. The problem is that the doctrine of salvation is emphasized out of proportion to the other doctrines of the Scriptures.

NOTES

1. Carl F. H. Henry, "Perspective for Social Action," *Christianity Today* (January 19, 1959), p. 11.

2. Addison H. Leitch, "The Primary Task of the Church," *Christianity Today* (October 15, 1956), p. 13.

3. Carl F. H. Henry, "What Is the Way to a New Society?" *Christianity Today* (November 26, 1956), p. 23.

4. Henry, "Perspective for Social Action," p. 11.

5. Henry, *The Uneasy Conscience*, p. 76.

3

Separation

OFTENTIMES IN evaluating a theological approach it is
not what is said that causes the greatest difficulty but
that which is left unsaid. Neoevangelicalism is not
completely silent on the doctrine of separation, but
neither is it very vocal. The very fact that the new evangelicalism proposes to mediate between liberalism and
fundamentalism precludes the fact that it will not be
very vociferous in favor of the doctrine of separation.
What the fundamentalist is said to have done in opposition to liberalism and the social gospel message, the
neoevangelical does in opposition to fundamentalism
with respect to the doctrine of separation. In both cases
there seems to be either a for or an against position
without any place for a proper balance. The
neoevangelicals do not deny that there is a place for
controversy today. They rather approach naively any
theological differences which may exist. They condone
remaining united with liberal denominations. Any
view of separation which some of them may have is
rarely supported with Scripture. Separation, especially
ecclesiastical separation, is considered a matter of conscience.

There are several reasons why they prefer this view to the view of most fundamentalists. Separation tends to produce a divisive spirit. A case in point is the splits in the Presbyterian Church. From the Presbyterian Church U.S.A. broke the Orthodox Presbyterian Church. From that the Bible Presbyterian movement was born, and from that came the group associated with Covenant Seminary in St. Louis. Separatists also tend to isolate themselves in a rather exclusivistic position. The fact of separation produces barriers which forbid profitable theological conversation between the conservative and nonconservative. Disagreement produces lack of communication, and lack of communication often produces bitterness and harshness of spirit.

Perhaps another reason for this antiseparatist position stems from the neoevangelical view of the church. Neoevangelicalism has little sympathy with any group which has left a denomination because it believed in unity enough to be concerned with the purity of its doctrine. While espousing belief in the local and universal church, the definite tendency is to emphasize the local to the seeming neglect of the universal. This is done, no doubt, to avoid the error of fundamentalism in being so involved in the universal invisible Body as to become unrealistic in regard to the present problems of the church here and now. This view is understandable since the neoevangelical stresses so strongly the belief that the church has a responsibility to apply the gospel to society.

Neoevangelicalism is not unaware of the perils both in independency and in ecumenicity.[1] This means that the neoevangelical position rejects the so-called extreme independency of organizations such as the American and International Councils of Christian Churches and the ecumenical approach of the National and World Councils of Churches. Neoevangelicalism does not accept strict independency because of its insistence upon what the neoevangelical calls lesser doctrines. It rejects the liberal ecumenical approach because it fails to give enough emphasis upon those doctrines which the neoevangelical considers important. The result of this two-fold rejection produces a view of unity which has a very minimum doctrinal basis for agreement.

The purposes and distinctive feature of the National Association of Evangelicals reveal the neglect of the doctrine of separation on the part of neoevangelicals. Paul Petticord, past president of the organization, shows what its purposes are not. The Association (which represents neoevangelicalism) was not born to combat someone or some organizations. Neither was the Association born to penetrate or infiltrate the National Council of Churches or organized for the purpose of dividing its forces. It was not born to be an evangelistic agency but a fellowship that encourages and stimulates evangelism through denominational channels to the local church or directly to the local church if its government makes such a provision. Strangely enough, the Association was not born to preempt the usage of the word *evangelical* as a substitute for the word *fundamentalism*. Finally, it was not born to become one church in an organic sense nor to do the work of the church.[2]

The purposes are positively stated in *The Strength of Spiritual Unity*, a small leaflet published by the Association. The purposes are as follows: (1) To foster fellowship and goodwill among all Bible-believing Christians in line with the prayer of Christ, "That they may be made perfect in one; and that the world may know that thou hast sent me"; (2) to provide a vehicle through which all believers in the Lord Jesus Christ may become united and articulate in matters of common interest and concern; (3) to establish a common front and a representation of evangelical interests and the promotion of evangelical truth against the inroads of modernism in Christian institutions and in public life; (4) to guard and promote religious freedom guaranteed us under our Constitution; and (5) to provide our constituents with services which will enable them to accomplish more quickly and efficiently the speedy evangelization of the world.

The distinctive feature of the National Association of Evangelicals is exactly the opposite of the American Council of Christian Churches as it relates to the National and World Councils of Churches, thus revealing the neglect of the doctrine of separation. The National Association of Evangelicals was not formed to combat or divide the forces of the National Council of Churches, but this is precisely what the American Council of Christian Churches was organized to do. The National Association of Evangelicals prefers to leave the decision of who or what is apostate up to the individual conscience. Membership in the National Association of Evangelicals is not dependent upon whether or not an individual or church is affiliated with the National or World Councils of Churches as it is in the American Council of Christian Churches.

Other expressions of neglect and denunciation of this doctrine will further substantiate the thesis of this chapter.

> The younger orthodox scholars are repudiating the separatist position, have repented of the attitude of solipsism, have expressed a willingness to re-examine the problems facing the theological world, have sought to return to the theological dialogue and have recognized the honesty and Christianity of some who hold views different from their own in some particulars.[3]

Neoevangelicals rejoice in all of this because to them these are signs of evangelical revival.

Carnell pointed out that he realized soon after he began his ministry that he was not a separatist by nature nor could he discover any Biblical warrant for the separatist position. He classified separatists with cultic orthodoxy as opposed to classical orthodoxy.[4] He accused the fundamentalist of inconsistency in thinking that possession of truth is the same thing as possession of virtue. He argued that the separatist has only one construction to put upon Paul's exhortation, "Wherefore come out from among them and be ye separate, saith the Lord" (2 Cor. 6:17). That construction is to physically withdraw from any communion that is not purely orthodoxy.[5]

Edward J. Young, late professor of Old Testament at Westminster Theological Seminary, challenged the neoevangelical neglect of and opposition to the doctrine of separation.

> With this attitude toward the church the New Evangelicalism has little or no sympathy. . . . Perhaps it is not incorrect to say that the New Evangelicalism would like to build up the church without any reference to the church. It stresses evangelism, and does not always show itself discriminate with respect to those whom it invites to support it. It stresses scholarship and education. In fact, it stresses just about everything except the all-important doctrine of the church, and the need for vigorous contending for the Faith. . . . Is then the New Evangelicalism the answer to the present-day situation? For our part we say no, and we say no emphatically. Here is a temporary phenomenon, and the sooner it passes, the better for the church. . . . There is much in Fundamentalism that is admirable, and if we were compelled to choose between Fundamentalism and New Evangelicalism, we should choose Fundamentalism without any hesitation.[6]

NOTES

1. "The Perils of Independency" and "The Perils of Ecumenicity."

2. Paul Petticord, *True Ecumenicity* (Wheaton, IL: National Association of Evangelicals, n.d.), pp. 9, 10.

3. Ockenga, "Resurgent Evangelical Leadership," p. 13.

4. Carnell, "Orthodoxy: Cultic vs. Classical," p. 378.

5. Carnell, *The Case for Orthodox Theology*, pp. 132, 133.

6. Edward J. Young, "Where Are We Going?" *The Presbyterian Guardian* (May—June 1959), cited by *The Sunday School Times* (January 28, 1961), p. 74.

4

Miscellaneous Doctrines

"FOR IF THE trumpet give an uncertain sound, who shall prepare himself to the battle?" (1 Cor. 14:8). There is a note of uncertainty and indefiniteness in the presentation of some of the doctrines of neoevangelicalism. This vagueness expresses itself either in a lack of sufficient presentation or in an uncertain presentation. This is not to imply that the new evangelicalism does not touch upon the areas which shall be mentioned. Neither is it to imply that all of the presentations are vague and indefinite. The reasons why the subjects which follow are considered areas of vagueness are because of the lack of essential uniformity of agreement within the leadership and because there is a seeming avoidance of the details associated with these subjects.

Take, as the first example, the doctrine of eschatology (last things). There is an unnecessary amount of fluidity and elasticity in the neoevangelicals' presentation of the program of God for the future. Only the broad aspects of God's program are discussed with any degree of uniformity. Such things as the second coming of Christ and future judgment are considered major and determinative (and even these are not always explained). Other areas of eschatology are considered as fine details and thus do not allow for dogmatism.

Flexibility in major areas of eschatology (millennialism, tribulationism and dispensationalism) is both serious and dangerous. It is serious because it produces bewilderment and uncertainty. It is dangerous because eschatology not only relates to the future but to the present as well. Neoevangelicalism proceeds cautiously, and rightly so, in pronouncing with certainty upon that which the Scripture is not clear. Perhaps this cautious spirit has been overworked, however. There are areas in which definite decisions must be made because these major areas determine the entire course of a theological system. The essential eschatological interpretations are not merely speculations to fascinate the human intellect; they are rooted in hermeneutical (interpretational) principles. They lie at the basis of either a literal or allegorical interpretation of Scripture.

Eschatological interpretations have a definite bearing upon many of the other doctrines which one holds. One's entire system of theology, view of history, interpretation of Scripture, view of the church as an organism and as an organization in relation to other organizations, and view of Biblical theology is determined to a great extent by his view of eschatology. Eschatological items are clamoring for attention today and cannot be avoided or minimized, especially since the optimistic utopian views of the liberal were shattered by the world wars. The present threats to survival also draw attention to eschatology.

In the structure of the new evangelicalism, eschatology is treated as somewhat peripheral. It becomes rather secondary and not primary.

> Contemporary evangelicalism needs . . . to restudy eschatological convictions for a proper perspective which will not unnecessarily dissipate evangelical strength in controversy over secondary positions, in a day when the significance of the primary insistences is international.[1]

Yet, this same evangelical theologian, who is to the right of center in the new evangelicalism, quite forcefully calls his other evangelical brethren to a restudy of eschatology. He calls for a balance between the modernist theology, which neglected doctrines related to the end times, and extreme fundamentalism, which cheapened and distorted those doctrines by datesetting and unwarranted identifications and isolations of future events from the here and now. He stresses the importance of eschatology and presents the various contending views as live options.[2]

The presentation of opposing schools of thought in eschatology is done quite readily. In *Christianity Today*, December 24, 1956, two articles dealing with Palestine and the future of the Jews were given. The one was written by Oswald T. Allis, a confirmed amillennialist (one who does not believe in a literal Millennium), and the other by Wilbur Smith, a premillennialist (one who believes Christ will come and establish the Millennium promised in the Old Testament). Again, in *Eternity*, May 1957, the pretribulation rapture position was presented by John F. Walvoord and the posttribulation rapture position by George Ladd. Pretribulationism holds that the Lord will remove the church before the Great Tribulation, and posttribulationism believes the church will be preserved through the tribulation. In both *Christianity Today* and *Eternity* the choice is up to the reader. What does this produce? It produces uncertainty and bewilderment on the part of the neoevangelical constituency, both laymen and clergy. It must be determined what is basic in eschatology and in what areas there will be room for disagreement.

Perhaps the rather widespread postmillennial views within neoevangelicalism explain the optimistic view of the church which is usually presented. Certainly, if Christ will not return until the Millennium has been established, either through man's efforts or through the universal preaching of the gospel, the church does not face a period of increasing apostasy but rather an increasing period of faithfulness in the proclamation of the gospel. This may help to explain the desire of the neoevangelical for the church to apply its message to the social scene. The sooner the gospel has been taken to the ends of the earth and has been effective in altering society, the sooner the return of Christ to the kingdom which man has established either by himself in social reform or through the preaching of the gospel of Christ. This is the position of some in the movement. Still others are amillennial in their eschatology. This lack of clarity and emphasis is surprising since eschatology was one of the doctrines which was to be stressed in *Christianity Today.*[3]

Another area of vagueness, which will only be touched upon here, is the relation of science to Scripture. How concessive ought the evangelical be to science? This question is not answered with uniformity by the leaders of neoevangelicalism. That a cleavage exists between science and religion is admitted by all. The futility of perpetuating that cleavage is also acknowledged. What is not agreed upon is the peril of compromising the cleavage. The threshold evolution of Edward John Carnell and the progressive creation of Bernard Ramm were questioned by Carl F. H. Henry because of their semantic delusion and false hope which they engender to gain a truce between science and religion. Henry's prospect for transcending the cleavage is a reconciliation through repentance and faith.[4]

Vagueness in this area is further aided by many articles which have appeared in popular religious magazines, articles such as "What Christian Colleges Teach About Creation," *Christianity Today* (June 17, 1977); "What Does Genesis Have To Do With Genes?" *His* (April 1975); "Social Science: Friend or Foe?" *His* (October 1976); "Science and Logic With Key to the Scriptures," *Eternity* (October 1977). Such articles leave more questions unanswered than are answered. The validity of the appearance of these types of articles is not being questioned, but the indecisiveness and uncertainty with which they conclude is fraught with serious problems. There seems to be an abundance of unnecessary attempts to reconcile the Bible with science. The changeableness of science and the stability of the Bible must be pondered deeply before concessions are made to science.

Surprisingly enough, with all the attention which neoevangelicals give to the matter of unity and ecumenism, there is still a lack of precision on this popular subject. There is general agreement that the prayer of Christ, "that they may be one," involves a visible church unity. The doctrine of unity is stressed and so is the impossibility of believers ever being in total agreement. What is vague in this connection is the precise area of basic doctrinal agreement.

What are the bare essentials necessary for union? Some would limit this to belief in Christ as Son of God. Others would include the Trinity and substitutionary atonement of Christ. These basic requirements, however, do not go much beyond the doctrinal statements of the liberal ecumenical movement. Neoevangelicalism finds itself in a somewhat strange position because it criticizes ecumenism and also rejects strict independency.

Ecumenism is chided for majoring on minors and independency for minoring on majors. Independency produces divisiveness, refuses to communicate with those in disagreement and assumes individualism. Ecumenism stops short of accepting the whole Bible upon which it bases its doctrine of unity. The ecumenist has not settled the nature of unity and must deal with the danger of the ecclesiasticism of the Roman Catholic type.[5] Both neoevangelicalism and fundamentalism would do well to clarify their interpretation of the Lord's prayer, "That they all may be one; as thou, Father, art in me, and I in thee, that they also may be one in us: that the world may believe that thou hast sent me" (John 17:21).

Then, too, there is an alarming vagueness in the doctrine of man. The vagueness in this area is due to almost complete neglect of the doctrine of total depravity. Whenever the sinfulness of man is touched upon, the possibility of victory over the state of sinfulness is stressed more than the fact of the deplorable state. Total depravity (the belief that man is born in sin and unable in and of himself to merit God's favor) is not denied by the neoevangelical. In fact, there is every reason to believe that he accepts it, especially since he stresses the necessity for individual salvation. This would be unnecessary were man not in need of such a redemption. The vagueness does not come, therefore, in a denial but in a lack of emphasis. It is not to be expected that every issue of *Christianity Today* and other publications should carry articles on depravity. But it does seem fair to expect a movement which claims to present historical Christianity and to be aligned with creedal Christianity to say more than has been said. Even in books such as *The Case for Orthodox Theology; Contemporary Evangelical Thought; The Christian View of Science and Scripture;* and *Evangelical Responsibility in Contemporary Theology* where there was not only opportunity but real need to present the scriptural view of man's sinfulness, there is only a scant presentation.

No doubt the neoevangelical's desire to stress man's responsibility in the social and intellectual arenas has caused vagueness in this crucial doctrine.

NOTES

1. Henry, *The Uneasy Conscience,* p. 57.
2. Carl F. H. Henry, "The Trumpet of the Lord," *Christianity Today* (June 10, 1957), pp. 20-23.
3. Carl F. H. Henry, "Why *Christianity Today?*" *Christianity Today* (October 15, 1956), p. 20.
4. Carl F. H. Henry (ed.), *Contemporary Evangelical Thought* (Great Neck, NY: Channel Press, 1957), pp. 247-257.
5. "The Perils of Independency" and "The Perils of Ecumenicity."

Part III

DIFFICULTIES

1

Uniting Conservatives

THE NEOEVANGELICAL sees three basic needs today. These three form the purpose for the new approach in evangelicalism. The first of these, which will be dealt with in this chapter, is the need for a united conservative front through which the gospel can be presented. The conservative ranks are much too fragmented to convince the world of our love for each other. The second basic need which the neoevangelical sees is the need to bring orthodoxy back into the arena as a live option for a world-life view. The need which constantly keeps harassing the neoevangelical is the need to make orthodoxy respectable. Finally, there is an honest desire in all of this to please the Lord and to fulfill the human obligations in the most acceptable manner. These last two desires will be discussed subsequently. One cannot read the neoevangelical publications without seeing and admiring these honest intentions. The question is, How well has the movement succeeded in accomplishing these?

Sad, but true, and the fundamentalist need not gloat over this, conservatives have not been united. As a matter of fact, it is quite evident in the minds of some that conservatism has been further divided as a result of the neoevangelical approach. Divisions have blurred the effectiveness of fundamentalism, and this must be confessedly admitted. Yet, some conservatives fear that the new evangelicalism is "a trend which may not only lead to another division, but one which will be the deepest and most disastrous of all."[1] John F. Walvoord of Dallas Theological Seminary sees no advancement for the cause of Christ in the use of the term *evangelical* as opposed to *fundamentalism*. In fact, "the term *evangelical* lends itself to manipulation by the modern liberal confusing both laity and clergy."[2]

Charles C. Ryrie, also of Dallas Theological Seminary, has evidenced a hesitancy to accept the universal condemnations of fundamentalism by the neoevangelicals. Ryrie pointed out that Henry in his *Christian Personal Ethics* did not practice what he preached about love because he placed unjust accusations upon fundamentalism.[3] He also rated the neoevangelical publication defending orthodoxy, *The Case for Orthodox Theology,* by Edward John Carnell, as running a poor third with its two companion volumes on liberal and neo-orthodox theology. "It fails in what is not said in the book, and it fails in certain unorthodox statements which are made."[4] Ryrie is disturbed not only with what was left unsaid and with the severe beating which fundamentalism received but also because of the harsh, bitter spirit which pervades its pages.

Individuals who speak for and represent various church groups have also expressed dissatisfaction with the new evangelical approach. The following is not to be construed as an indication that the entire movements which these represent have condemned neoevangelicalism. It merely reveals what some in responsible places of leadership think and how they evaluate this new approach. This is further substantiation that conservatives have not been united by the neoevangelical approach. Especially significant is the fact that this dissatisfaction is so widespread among those with differing denominational, interdenominational and nondenominational affiliations. The leadership of the General Association of Regular Baptist Churches has candidly rejected the new evangelicalism. A former national representative's unpublished paper, "A New Peril in the Last Days," was an examination of the new trend in evangelical theology and a rejection of it. Other articles appearing in the Association's monthly *Baptist Bulletin* reveal dissatisfaction with the new evangelicalism.

Leaders and voices for the Independent Fundamental Churches of America have also rejected basic presuppositions of the neoevangelical approach. A former editor of *Voice* magazine, which represents the I.F.C.A., expressed deep concern and distrust of the new evangelicalism. He stated very clearly why the I.F.C.A. is separate from the National Association of Evangelicals. The two reasons are the attitude of the N.A.E. toward apostasy and its broad doctrinal position.[5]

William A. Ashbrook spoke very strongly against the new evangelicalism in the *Voice* and in a booklet entitled *Evangelicalism: the New Neutralism.* He identified the movement as one born of compromise, nurtured on pride of intellect, growing on appeasement of evil, and doomed by the judgment of God's Word. James A. Stewart, an international evangelist of fundamentalist persuasion, vowed that fundamentalists should not cooperate with modernists in "Ecumenical Evangelism."[6] Glen A. Lehman summarized the I.F.C.A.'s position in his evaluation of Harold John Ockenga's Founder's Day address on January 9, 1960, at Wheaton College: "His New Evangelicalism does not satisfy the hunger of a hundred thousand hearts."[7]

The Bible Presbyterian movement has certainly not accepted the new evangelicalism. The editor of the *Christian Beacon* declared that the new evangelicalism represents the dismal compromise of the day.[8] Too, the sharpest and most critical review of Carnell's book *The*

Case for Orthodox Theology came from the pen of J. Oliver Buswell in the *Bible Presbyterian Reporter*, December 1959.

An element of Methodism has also entered in the attack. Shuler registered protest in his article, "The New Evangelicalism," in the *Methodist Challenge*, September 1958.

What is even more substantiating evidence of the failure of the new evangelicalism to unite conservatives is the growing concern to hold the line among those within the movement. Neoevangelicalism has not only failed to unite all conservatives, it has even failed to unite its own constituency. Through personal correspondence and conversation with individuals who are usually identified as neoevangelicals, it has been discovered that not all is well and unified even within the camp. There is a growing tendency on the part of some within the neoevangelical school of thought to view with caution the rather broad concessions which some of their brethren are making for the cause of unity and respectability.

Rather than uniting conservatives, there is further division in the ranks. While the leaders of these movements and schools can visualize clearly the issues involved, the ordinary layman does not. He only believes that things are now as they always have been, and usually any warning on the part of pastor or denominational leaders is interpreted as bigotry and unnecessary quibbling. The layman cannot see the danger, thus there is some unrest and uncertainty in many conservative quarters.

NOTES

1. McClain, "Is Theology Changing . . . ?" p. 124.
2. John F. Walvoord, "What's Right About Fundamentalism?" *Eternity* (June 1957).
3. Charles C. Ryrie, review of *Christian Personal Ethics* by Carl F. H. Henry, *Bibliotheca Sacra* (January 1958), p. 85.

4. Charles C. Ryrie, "A Trilogy of Theology," *Bibliotheca Sacra* (January 1960), p. 15.

5. Ernest Pickering, "Why the I.F.C.A. Does Not Belong to the N.A.E.," *Voice* (September 1957), p. 5.

6. James A. Stewart, "Ecumenical Evangelism," *Voice* (April 1957), p. 6.

7. Glen A. Lehman, "Societal Application of the Gospel," *Voice* (May 1960), p. 2.

8. "Fundamentalist Failure," *Christian Beacon* (December 18, 1958), p. 8.

2

Making Orthodoxy Respectable

THE EXTREMES and inadequacies of fundamentalism combined with the denials of liberalism and neo-orthodoxy had in the minds of the neoevangelicals displaced orthodoxy as a major alternative in theology. It is the desire of the new evangelicalism to present orthodoxy once again in such a way that it will be brought back into the mainstream of theological current and again become a live option. Ockenga expressed the ambitions of the neoevangelical very succinctly:

> He desires to win a new respectability for orthodoxy in the academic circles by producing scholars who can defend the faith on intellectual ground. . . . He intends to restate his position carefully and cogently so that it must be considered in the theological dialogue.[1]

There is a desire to please the liberal, not by denying any of the cardinal doctrines of the fundamentalist but by being less polemic and more positive and loving. The assumption is that the time is ripe for mutual confession of the past and for the sharing of theological viewpoints so that orthodoxy may become less objectionable to those outside its ranks. Worthy as this ambition may be, it is beset with serious difficulties.

It must always be remembered that orthodoxy is objectionable to the nonconservative, not merely because of how it is presented but because of what it is. The message of orthodoxy is the real cause of rejection and not simply the method which has been used in the proclamation. Has this new emphasis and presentation of evangelicalism been successful in making orthodoxy respectable? Perhaps that is expecting too much from a relatively young movement. Are there *any signs* of accomplishment in this connection? In brief, what impression has new evangelicalism made upon liberalism and neoorthodoxy? Who has gained the most from the new approach? Has the elimination and alteration of certain aspects of fundamentalism been worth the gains?

For objective answers to these questions the liberal and neoorthodox must be allowed to speak for themselves. An investigation of the attitude and response of the enemy is very disheartening. There must be no pride in rejoicing in another's failures; yet, neoevangelicalism has failed in its attempt to gain status orthodoxy perhaps even more tragically than in its attempt to unite conservatives. A survey of *The Christian Century*, a mouthpiece of liberalism, reveals that the liberals think the neoevangelicals are quite benighted. The remainder of this chapter is not written—and should not be read—with the I-told-you-so attitude, for this is a discouraging report in view of the intended accomplishments.

Attacks from liberalism and neoorthodoxy center largley, though not exclusively, upon Billy Graham. No doubt this is true because the neoevangelicals have claimed him as the evangelist representing neo-evangelicalism. Also the liberal considers Graham a symbol and rallying center for many Protestants. Many of the criticisms which nonconservatives hurl at him are not true, and those which have some basis of truth are sorely lacking in love—the thing about which the liberal often talks the most and does the least. These attitudes are given here for the sole purpose of revealing the difficulty and failure so that it may become evident that the liberal does not want merely a changed wrapping; he has, and wants others to have, another product.

Surprisingly enough, liberalism has been quite vocal in expressing dissatisfaction with the new evangelicalism or what they call "the contemporary fundamentalist renascence." One writer feels that Graham, who represents the fundamentalist renascence, does not preach the whole gospel. He confines the gospel to that part which focuses on sin, repentance and the forgiveness of God.

> It is high time for Protestantism to ask: Can this be done? That is, can it be done without actually misrepresenting the Christian Faith? . . . Are we not bound to say that this truncated evangelism is giving to the world and the church itself a distorted, shallow, inflated and unbiblical conception of Christianity?[2]

In the same article the writer goes on to judge rather severely the National Association of Evangelicals:

> Some forty fundamentalist groups are now federated in an organization called the "National Association of Evangelicals." That term "evangelical" has been adopted avowedly to offset the prejudice which the term "fundamentalism" had acquired in its earlier, intensely controversial period. Thus the noblest word in the vocabulary of Christian evangelism has been raped by its association with this un-evangelical deviation from New Testament Christianity.[3]

With all the concern and attention which the new evangelicalism gives to the social scene, one would expect the liberal to be delighted; yet, they are anything but impressed. After evaluating the effect of the crusade in Australia, they criticized Graham for a lack of social content in his messages.

> The almost complete absence of any social content in the message meant that the "principalities and powers" of Australian society went unchallenged. . . . Dr. Graham's message takes too little account of the world revolution. . . . Therefore he failed to touch the hard core of resistance to Christianity in Australia, as for example in the trade unions.[4]

Another makes a rather unusual comparison of personalities in expressing the cultural lack in neo-evangelicalism.

> The "ethical lag" in the church's social thinking and teaching is all the more painfully evident in the woeful deficiencies of the gospel as presented by Norman Vincent Peale and Billy Graham. Many of us feel that these brethren, be they ever so "sincere," are preaching a mutilated message, a truncated gospel, particularly because of their naivete in the face of an alluring and ensnaring culture.[5]

Quite frequently, the liberals, while they recognize the term *new evangelicalism*, think of the movement only as a resurgence of fundamentalism. As far as they are concerned, fundamentalism was outdated, outmoded and defeated with the exception of a few semiliterate stick-in-the-muds who existed in certain cultural backwaters but were not taken very seriously. They looked at fundamentalism somewhat as society looks at an ignoramus—pitifully beyond help. The more concerned liberal accepts as a missionary challenge the responsibility of informing and alerting his brethren of the devastating outcome of the new evangelicalism type of evangelism. They see behind the revivalistic efforts of Graham a development to which most of the churches are blind.

> It is the attempted revival of fundamentalism as a major factor in Protestant life. . . . Through skillful manipulation of means and persons, including a well publicized association with the President of the United States [Dwight Eisenhower at the time] fundamentalistic forces are now in a position aggressively to exploit the churches.[6]

In other words, the liberal has awakened to the fact that he is being taken.

Liberal churchmen who have supported Graham's crusades out of a sense of desperation are no less desperate now than they were a decade ago. Generally speaking, liberals feel that there are better ways to spend millions of dollars than in mass evangelism. As far as they are concerned, the liberal churches must do to revivalism what they did to the old modernism—go beyond it.

It seems as though the intended result of neoevangelicalism is working in reverse, and to this neoevangelicals cannot afford to be oblivious. Instead of leading the liberal to orthodoxy, the new evangelicalism is making him careful not to return to that from which he was liberated through liberalism in its battle with fundamentalism.

> Such a confrontation ought not to lead nonfundamentalist seminarians to return to the liberalism of the 1920's, but it might, if critically entered into, prevent them from falling into a state in which they could semiconsciously slip back toward the borderland of those authoritarian patterns from which liberalism once set us free.[7]

Both the context and consequences of the new evangelicalism's evangelism have been criticized by the liberal. The context is one of coercion and threat that those who do not cooperate are causing a division in the ecumenical fellowship. Thus, many ministers and churches are unsympathetic but give formal support to the crusades as the choice of a lesser wrong. The resultant consequences are judged by the liberal because after the revival the fundamentalist groups and churches do not intend to participate in the church federation after the team leaves town.

The consequences of such cooperation are also very costly, reasons the liberal. Fundamentalism has always been a divisive movement, and the liberal does not see any change in this direction in the new evangelicalism.

The lack of connecting the gospel with the Christian faith as a whole is felt to be grossly misrepresenting the task of the church. A full-orbed challenge of God's unfailing forgiveness and love to all who share in the fellowship of the church is lacking. Mass evangelism is charged with leaving the new convert to nurse his impulse in the subjectivity of his self-consciousness, and this is not pleasing to the Spirit of God.[8]

The neoevangelicals have hoped that the production of scholars who could defend orthodoxy on intellectual grounds would cause the nonevangelicals to listen respectfully to what orthodoxy has to say. Liberals have been surprised somewhat to hear from evangelicals who have had an education which meets with their approval. They are in a dither as they listen, however, because they see contradictions and illogic in the new evangelicalism. As a matter of fact, they ridicule the fundamentalist logic as it relates to the inerrancy of the Bible. By *fundamentalist* here they mean new evangelical, for they often use the terms interchangeably.[9] In a review of *The Case for Orthodox Theology* one writer praised Carnell for criticizing fundamentalism but complained that Carnell's type of orthodoxy was diverted from the main task today.[10] Another liberal was even more vigorous in his criticism of Carnell's view of Scripture displayed in *The Case for Orthodoxy.*

> Carnell feels that . . . even though the Old Testament appears to contradict both science and itself, and though much of its content lacks revelatory power . . . we must believe that *in some sense* the original writings were free from error. This sense *may* be that an inspired author correctly copied an inaccurate document! Obviously, if such an interpretation of inspiration is accepted, the fact that a statement appears in Scripture is no grounds for believing it to be true. Hence, the only value of the doctrine of inspiration appears to lie in being loyal to what is supposed to be the view of Jesus.[11]

American neoorthodoxy, in the person of Reinhold Neibuhr, has also contributed its share of criticism of

Graham and the new evangelicalism which he represents. Niebuhr took Graham to task for his literalism
and individualism.[12] He, too, criticized the deficient
societal impact of Graham's ministry. He even challenged Graham to validate his message by applying it
to racial problems.

If these criticisms and this difficulty bring joy to
anyone, then he is guilty of a worse sin than could ever
be committed by those who are attempting to communicate with all nonconservatives. In brief, the liberal
and neoorthodox reactions to the new evangelicalism
range from sheer neglect to mere recognition and harsh
criticism. They have been accused of using sincere but
faulty means to reach their goal. They are tabbed as
hypocritical, unethical and downright dishonest in
some instances.

Actually, the new evangelicalism finds itself on the
horns of a dilemma. Its message has not been acceptable to the hard core of old-time fundamentalism and
some to the right of center in neoevangelicalism;
neither has it been respected to any great extent by
liberalism and neoorthodoxy. Some quarters of fundamentalism have been very vocal and sometimes
quick in their criticisms of neoevangelicalism, but
liberalism quite generally has been exceedingly harsh
and bitter. A paradoxical situation exists with these
two opponents of neoevangelicalism. Fundamentalism
fears the new evangelicalism has been far too concessive, while liberalism fears that there will be a harvest
of confusion, division and a paralyzing consequence
for those who cooperate and fall for the new evangelical
line. The ecumenical attempts of the neoevangelical are
considered very superficial to the liberal and are endeavored only to match his ecumenical theology.

Perhaps the new evangelicalism would do well to
reevaluate its aims and purposes in light of the apostle
Paul. In spite of all his intellectual training, his presentation of the gospel was unacceptable to most of the
religious leaders of his day. As a matter of fact, they

thought he had become insane and the gospel was anything but respectable for them; rather, it was offensive. His own converts were also among those who rejected him. This is not to suggest the abolishment of education; God forbid. The gospel must be presented clearly, defensibly and intelligently. It is to suggest, though, that however well the gospel may be restated, it will always be offensive to the unbeliever because of the stigma of the cross, which is the heart of the gospel message.

NOTES

1. Ockenga, "Resurgent Evangelical Leadership," p. 14.

2. Charles Clayton Morrison, "The Past Foreshadows the Future," *The Christian Century* (March 5, 1958), p. 273.

3. Ibid.

4. Alan Walker, "Graham in Australia," *The Christian Century* (July 15, 1959), p. 823.

5. William H. Kirkland, "Needed: A 'Culture Ethic,' " *The Christian Century* (December 18, 1957), p. 1511.

6. "Fundamentalist Revival," *The Christian Century* (June 19, 1957), p. 749.

7. Arnold W. Hearn, "Fundamentalist Renascence," *The Christian Century* (April 30, 1958), p. 530.

8. Morrison, "The Past Foreshadows the Future," p. 273.

9. Marcius E. Taber, "Fundamentalist Logic," *The Christian Century*, (July 3, 1957), pp. 817ff.

10. "A Protestant Believes in God," *The Christian Century* (May 20, 1959), p. 603.

11. John B. Cobb, "A Panorama of Theologies," *Interpretation* (January 1960), p. 96.

12. Reinhold Niebuhr, "Literalism, Individualism and Billy Graham," *The Christian Century* (May 23, 1956).

3

Holding the Line

MOST CONSERVATIVE Christians think in terms of positive and negative, yes or no, black or white, for or against; but individuals associated with neo-evangelicalism cannot be that easily classified. There is a wide range of differences within what is usually considered neoevangelical circles. And this is precisely what causes such a serious difficulty from within the movement itself. Obviously, one does not expect unanimous agreement on every detail of doctrine and program. There will always be disagreements in any group as long as people are involved. In fact, some disagreement is healthy. However, there is serious disagreement in matters of vital importance among neoevangelicals. How much restating of the gospel is to be made? How much concession is there to be to the scientist and liberal theologian? In what areas may concessions be made without altering the message? What is the criterion for orthodoxy? Is the neoevangelical emphasis the Biblical emphasis? These are some of the perplexing questions which are plaguing those who are to the right of center in neoevangelicalism. There is considerable internal unrest and uncertainty. Perhaps the hesitations of some within the ranks and the often-times brutal castigation from those without will serve as a check to the new evangelical approach.

In addition to the human opposition, neo-evangelicalism must constantly evaluate its beliefs and practices in the light of the Word. Ultimately, the question is not, Have I pleased men? but, Have I been obedient to the heavenly call? Is the Lord satisfied? Have I been faithful to God's revelation? After all, there are troublesome passages which contradict some practices of the neoevangelical, and these must always haunt the honest and sincere.

From an objective perspective it looks as though much of the internal difficulty comes from the lack of a definitive doctrinal basis of agreement. Granted that neoevangelicals claim to believe all that fundamentalists believe, we have ample reason to question how widespread that doctrinal agreement is. Some do believe as the fundamentalist, but the number who do not is steadily increasing. Some of the most influential indicate uncertainty in some very central doctrines. Fundamentalism is basically a doctrinal position. The five fundamentals were considered determinative. These five fundamentals are no longer stressed by the neoevangelical. Maybe this helps to explain the fuzziness on the part of some. Neoevangelicalism is not a doctrinal position in the sense that fundamentalism is. Maybe there would be more agreement within if it were.

The sincerity of the neoevangelicals cannot be denied. To accuse them of some sort of sabotage or theological trickery would be immensely unjust and unfair. Sincerity alone, however, does not solve problems, neither does it make success out of failure or reconcile differences. The honest sincerity is observable in not a few of the leaders in their expressed concern for a holding of the line in areas that matter most.

No one can read the editorials and some of the feature articles in *Christianity Today* without recognizing that the editor is seeking to warn and alert the new evangelicalism of weakness, failure and impending danger. Then, too, certain neoevangelical publications deal frankly with internal difficulties and problems which face the new evangelicalism. In his *Evangelical Responsibility in Contemporary Theology*, Henry is careful to point out the limits and characteristics of evangelical cooperation with nonevangelical organizations set for the correcting of societal ills. He also emphasizes the need for an indispensable doctrinal basis for church unity. He pens a needy warning which is descriptive of his attitude and the attitudes of some others.

> We dare not own any other authority over life and deed but the living God. We dare not own any other God than the righteous and merciful God revealed in Jesus Christ. We dare not own another Christ but Jesus of Nazareth, the Word become flesh who now by the Spirit is the exalted head of the body of believers. We dare not own any other Spirit than the Spirit who has breathed out Scripture through chosen men, so that doubt may vanish about what God is saying to the Church and to the world.[1]

This comes as a very needed reaffirmation of what must be believed, and it is especially significant coming from a staunch leader in the new evangelicalism.

There is some unrest within neoevangelicalism concerning the matter of ecumenicity and the National and World Councils of Churches. Some within the movement have not been satisfied to merely encourage association with these liberally dominated organizations but are now speaking somewhat favorably of their programs and aims. This has completely shocked some other neoevangelicals and has even caused the resignation of positions by some to associate with other elements in conservatism with which they can find more agreement. Some neoevangelicals are evidently so enamored with church unity that this goal takes precedence over other doctrines, including the authority of Scripture. William Culbertson was right when he affirmed that "hobnobbing too closely with the enemy has always cost the cause of Christianity much more than it ever gained."[2]

It is in the area of Biblical authority that the most serious disagreement exists in neoevangelicalism. Professedly espousing an orthodox doctrine of Scripture, some err in practice by making Scripture subordinate to other considerations. They evidently do not believe the doctrine of Scripture is important enough to make an issue over so long as there is belief in the deity of Christ and His atoning work. Understandably, there are dissatisfactions with such concessions. In an article in *Christianity Today* entitled "The Word of God in Education," Frank Gaebelein expressed his alarm and concern in this connection.

> We should rejoice at the renaissance of good and enlightened scholarship among evangelicals which is sometimes called neo-evangelicalism. But at the same time we must not blink the evidence that there is current among some evangelicals a subtle erosion of the doctrine of the infallibility of Scripture that is highly illogical as well as dangerous. . . . Let us by all means redefine and restate the evangelical position but never at the cost of yielding any essential part of the authority of the Bible.[3]

A severe criticism and expression of internal difficulty over the authority of Scripture was stated in the Fall 1960 issue of the *Bulletin of the Evangelical Theological Society*. The article entitled "Hermeneutics as a Cloak for the Denial of Scripture" undoubtedly came as a shock to neoevangelicals. Especially was this true since Wheaton College, the school which J. Barton Payne, the author, represented at that time, has been categorized by some as having neoevangelical influences on its campus. The article was an excellent attempt to come to the defense of orthodoxy by means of the authority of Scripture, which area Carnell clouded so tragically in his book *The Case for Orthodox Theology*.

Payne sought to demonstrate three specific areas in

which Carnell strained hermeneutics to cover what Payne implied in the title of the article was Carnell's denial of Scripture. It must be readily admitted that Carnell raised more problems concerning the orthodox view of Scripture than he answered. Without question, his entire book and especially the chapter on "Authority" demonstrated how far one neoevangelical was willing to go in order to make a case for orthodoxy before the liberal and neoorthodox. Take as an example such a questionable statement as this: "The lower stages have to be read in the light of the higher, with the correction which the higher affords."[4] Perhaps a more questionable conclusion is his classification of Calvinism as cultic since it seldom appreciates the extent to which the New Testament ethic judges the truncated ethic of the Old Testament.[5]

Payne was very likely correct in assuming that Carnell and other scholars had good intentions to alleviate concern over certain of the Bible's difficulties and thus give the believer more assurance.

> But good intentions fail to obviate the following three facts: (1) Our anti-evangelical critics see more clearly than can some of us the incongruity of professing to believe in inerrancy while at the same time denying it in reference to the concrete data of Scripture. A consistent orthodoxy will warrant more respect than an obscurantist neoevangelicalism. (2) The propagation of the gospel depends upon a clear witness to its proper interpretation. . . . To condone invalid applications of the principles of its interpretation is to open the gates for views ranging from Romanism to Mormonism, which, we must recall, accepts the Bible as the Word of God, "as far as it is translated correctly" (articles of faith). (3) The authority of our Bible cannot long survive our disbelief in its contents.[6]

The three major difficulties of neoevangelicalism which have been presented in these chapters serve to illustrate the problems which exist without and within the movement. Evangelicalism has been further divided as a result of this new approach. Biblical orthodoxy is no more acceptable or respectable to its enemies now than it was in the presentation which fundamentalism made. Perhaps the last difficulty, discussed in this chapter, is the most serious of all because of the internal unrest. These difficulties may bring with them signs of improvement but they are certainly nothing over which to rejoice. It is something about which every child of God ought to pray.

The advances of the enemy make this the most vital hour for all conservatism to join in a scriptural proclamation and defense of the faith. Fundamentalism cannot afford to stand back in gleeful criticism of neoevangelicalism without a self-criticism because it, too, has its share of difficulties with which it must deal in order that it may be obedient to the whole counsel of God. The internal unrest may be an evidence that some neoevangelicals are growing too rapidly. Have they outgrown their fundamentalist forefathers? God grant that they shall take heed to the warnings of friends and foes lest they lose their Biblical moorings.

NOTES

1. Henry, *Evangelical Responsibility*, pp. 85, 86.
2. William Culbertson, cited by McClain, "Is Theology Changing. . . ?" p. 124.
3. Frank Gaebelein, "The Word of God in Education," *Christianity Today* (May 9, 1960), p. 7.
4. Carnell, *The Case for Orthodox Theology*, pp. 52, 53.
5. Ibid., p. 55.
6. Barton J. Payne, "Hermeneutics as a Cloak for the Denial of Scripture," *Bulletin of the Evangelical Theological Society* (Fall 1960), p. 99.

Part IV

DANGERS

1

Dangers in Neoevangelicalism

IN SOME RESPECTS dangers are like the proverbial bad penny—they always show up. The problem is they are not always recognizable by those who can correct or avoid them. Sometimes an outsider must don the role of a realistic prophet in order to startle the insider into reality. The results of such an outside observation may be altogether too pessimistic and cause rebellion from those more closely associated with that which is being criticized. Such a reaction may result from the bold presentation of serious dangers in neoevangelicalism which are presented in this chapter. These are dangers and weaknesses which now exist in neoevangelicalism. Their resultant outcome will depend upon the precautionary measures which are taken against them. They are written in love and with a spirit of concern and ought not be misinterpreted as rock-hurling. The writer does not claim to have the foretelling gift of prophecy but is only reflecting upon history and the present circumstances. Neither does the writer revel in the content of these proclamations and "prophecies," nor does he anticipate that the reader should. The seriousness of the dangers forbids such sins. The order in which the dangers are listed is purely arbitrary and, therefore, without any intention of indicating the order of importance.

Unrealistic Optimism

Extreme pessimists seldom find a welcome in any crowd and rightly so. Optimists are much more welcome and that is understandable. Realists, however, though they may not always be welcome, have a ministry to perform in checking unrealistic optimisms. Extreme pessimism stifles progress, while unrealistic optimism produces a false impression of circumstances.

An unhealthy impression is current today as a result of the neoevangelical's acceptance of the contemporary return to "Biblical theology." The careful student of contemporary theology will observe, however, that neoevangelicalism has not accepted on a wholesale basis the "returns" of the liberal and neoorthodox. The student will find that men such as Carl F. H. Henry criticize the liberal and neoorthodox returns to "Biblical theology" for some of their inadequacies. The average layman is not a student, however, and the difficulty is heightened when other neoevangelicals fail to reveal the shortcomings and failures of these movements. The impression usually given is that the evangelical must rejoice in the "conversion" of the liberal and neoorthodox. Even Henry, though he shows the failure of neoorthodoxy to affirm the evangelical position, leaves the impression that Barth is to be praised for the extent to which he moved toward orthodoxy. Henry explains how Barth speaks of the Word of God, the virgin birth, deity of Christ, sinlessness of Christ and second coming of Christ. Henry does conclude, "It would be an overstatement to imply that in the recovery of these doctrinal emphases Barth and the neoorthodox theologians return in all essentials to an historic evangelical exposition. That is not the case."[1]

What is necessary and would have added to Henry's discussion is an explanation of the neoorthodox

view of history. Their view of history explains how 131
they can speak of the doctrines of evangelicalism and
yet not believe them as the evangelical does. Neoorthodoxy does not accept the Christian interpretation
of history. Barth's terms for understanding history are
"historiographic" and "unhistoriographic." The unhistoriographic aspect relates primarily to creation and
means that it is not to be understood in creaturely
terms. History which stands in an indirect relation to
God is called historiographic, i.e., man. All of this simply means that records may be true, but if the event
stands in a direct relation to God, it is beyond history,
i.e., Adam.

Brunner, another neoorthodox leader, used the
term *primal history* to explain his view. This he contrasted to real history. For him, then, there was a history behind history. The one operated on the plane of
faith; the other on the plane of sight. Before the monu-
ments become understandable and credible records
appear, everything is in the realm of primal history and
the plane of faith. The creation and fall, for example,
would appear in this area.

Now, what means all of this when the neoorthodox
speaks of doctrine with an evangelical "ring" or
"rigor," to use Henry's terms? It means that more emphasis is placed upon the faith of historical happenings
than upon the fact of those happenings. Take for example, the creation of the first man called Adam, his position in a garden called Eden, his relation to a woman
called Eve—these are all denied as factual. The faith of
these things? Yes. The fact of them? No.

The same criticism applies to the neoevangelical
evaluation of neoliberalism. Though it is acknowledged
that present-day liberalism fails to embrace evangelicalism, its orthodox language is praised.

> One of the remarkable turns in the theology of the
> recent past is that theologians who once shared
> the liberal viewpoint and dogmatically excluded
> from the essence of the Christian religion doc-

trines like the deity of Christ, His virgin birth, substitutionary atonement, and bodily resurrection, now confess that this perspective was gained from a standpoint of secular unbelief. The marked swing to a greater theological conservatism today involves increasing emphasis on a central and indispensable core of Christian doctrine.[2]

What the neoevangelical fails to do, and herein lies the danger, is to portray in terms equally as clear the contemporary liberal foundation. The foundation upon which neoliberalism builds is precisely that foundation upon which old liberalism built. The Bible as infallible and authoritative is still rejected. Hence, all the orthodox language is like so much high-sounding nonsense because the meaning of such language is far from orthodox. Actually, then, the only gain which neoorthodoxy and neoliberalism have brought to the evangelical is the resurgence of evangelical terminology but not evangelical belief. It is alarming indeed in light of the neoorthodox view of history and the neoliberal foundation to find statements which are rather complimentary of these movements and condemnatory of the evangelical who does not accept them. Some go so far as to call for the acceptance of neoorthodox men as Christians. Such statements are much too broad and unqualified.

The usual neoevangelical evaluation of liberalism gives the impression that the battle between truth and error is over. While admitting certain basic fallacies in the new liberal approach, there seems to be an undefined acceptance of the liberal's "conversion" in other areas. Language which speaks highly of liberalism and neoorthodoxy and decries fundamentalism leaves the layman with a false impression. Neoevangelicals speak frequently of the decay of the Wellhausen hypothesis and the return to Biblical theology. In surveys of the change which world conditions and neoorthodoxy brought upon liberalism, they speak optimistically of many who genuinely returned to a conservative faith.

Further adding to the unrealistic optimism is the appearance of articles such as "Orthodox Agony in the World Council," "Evangelical Penetration of the WCC" and "Evangelical Gains in WCC" in *Christianity Today*. Again, such articles imply to the uninformed layman the "victories" of evangelicalism. He is led to believe that evangelicalism has finally triumphed and succeeded in converting its opponents, and, of course, this is not an accurate picture.

Doctrinal Neglect

Neoevangelicalism has areas of doctrinal emphasis, neglect and vagueness. Yet, it must be understood here that neoevangelicalism is not basically a doctrinal position as fundamentalism was and still is. This is not to say that doctrines are not discussed. Some doctrines are discussed, but many are not stressed. A critical review of materials promoting the evangelical cause reveals that doctrine is not sufficiently important to cause a rift among the brethren and with those who are not brethren. Granting the neoevangelical his basic proposition and premise—that orthodoxy is to be made respectable at the liberal's theological table—it is understandable that doctrine will not take precedence on the neoevangelical agenda. Whenever doctrines are discussed, they are presented with an unnecessary amount of indefiniteness and uncertainty. This is not true of all the evangelical doctrines but it is of some, and some of the fundamentals at that. Take, for example, the doctrinal uncertainty produced in such a vital area as the virgin birth of Christ, or the great deal of fluidity of interpretation in the area of eschatology.[3] This neglect of doctrine also evidences itself in the proposal for a Christian university. Such a university is to give a statement which will provide the adequacies for a world-life view in a day of doctrinal decline. Yet, it is admitted that assent to the articles of the Apostles' Creed is all that could be expected of its faculty.[4]

Fundamentalism is criticized sharply for its doctrinal emphasis which is said to have caused neglect of the social application of Christianity to the world. "Concentration on a few points of doctrine to the exclusion of ethics has also brought fundamentalism under discredit. . . . Failure to develop a system of Christian ethics for all phases of life proved harmful."[5] It is a bit paradoxical that neoevangelicalism should neglect doctrine, the very thing in which fundamentalism is criticized for being extreme.

Doctrinal emphasis is replaced by an emphasis upon evangelical cooperation. This is a specific goal of neoevangelicalism. Steps were taken toward its realization in the formation of the National Association of Evangelicals. This evangelical cooperation is often accomplished in a given situation or area because doctrine is neglected or at least relegated to a subservient position for the sake of unity. This is especially noticeable in the evangelistic efforts of neoevangelicalism where frequently little discretion is used of those with whom it joins hands. These efforts have as a basis for association a very minimal doctrinal agreement.

Another emphasis replacing the doctrinal emphasis of fundamentalism is the societal impact. Neoevangelicalism throbs with a desire to change society. The degree of the change and the method of its accomplishment are not always agreed upon, but all hope for a new world order of some description. Fundamentalism, no doubt, failed many times to apply its message to the social scene, but neoevangelicalism emphasizes this responsibility to the neglect of others. The neoevangelical is quite willing to join hands with any existing worthwhile effort in the improvement of society. The fact that such existing social reform movements may not be set in a redemptive context does not hinder neoevangelical zeal and support.

Love also replaces the doctrinal emphasis of the fundamentalist. Carnell was clear on this point:

> While we must be solicitious about *doctrine*,
> Scripture says that our primary business is

love.... While doctrine illuminates the plan of salvation, the mark of a true disciple is *love,* not doctrine. Scripture teaches this with such clarity and force that only a highly developed sense of religious pride could miss it. "And if I have prophetic powers, and understand all mysteries and all knowledge, and if I have all faith, so as to remove mountains, but have not love, I am nothing" (1 Cor. 13:2). Doctrine puffs up, love edifies.[6]

It seems necessary for this truth to be seasoned with a proper balance of other commandments in the Word of God. In addition to the all-important love which must characterize every believer, there must also be a holding fast of the faithful Word and an earnest contending for *the faith,* and that involves a body of truth or doctrine.

Substituting for the Essential

A third existing danger in neoevangelicalism is the danger of putting knowledge in the place of faith rather than as a corollary to it. Tremendous importance is placed upon intellectualism. Intentionally or unintentionally, the impression conveyed is that intellectualism and academic excellence are to be achieved simply for the sake of its own contribution. In other words, academic achievement is divorced oftentimes from faith. Faith is placed on a plane of lesser importance, while knowledge is placed on a higher plane. Because of the emphasis upon intellectualism, knowledge is often substituted for faith. In another connection entirely, but apropos to the matter under discussion, this danger has been exploited.

Around a fact originally apprehended in the simplicity of Christian faith there gradually grows up, as the result of this process, a scaffolding or encasement of protective formulations—abstruse, complex, scholastic—and the temptation is great to make the acceptance of these a substitute for faith itself. This is the real peril of intellectualism to which the Church is constantly exposed; and the remedy for it is the continual reversion to and habitual contemplation of, that living image of Christ in the Gospels in which all contrasts are harmonized—where the divine and human are seen in their *actual* union.[7]

This is not the time to decry wisdom and learning, but it is past the time to reassert the fact that intellectualism for the child of God must never become an end in itself. It is a means to the end of glorifying God, Who alone is to be worshiped, rather than the means. When intellectualism becomes the self-existent goal for the Christian scholar, he has lost his Biblical moorings, and his intellectualism becomes a militant enemy against his God-given faith. Whenever the Christian scholar prides himself in his intellectual abilities, he has sacrificed the most noble of Christian graces for a knowledge which by itself is lifeless and thereby powerless. Wisdom is like wealth in at least one essential; the possession of either or both is not the root of evil; but the love and adoration of either or both of them, for their intrinsic value alone, is a great provocation against God. Apostolic Christianity was not immersed with worldly learning and brilliance; it was bathed in the simplicity and expectancy of faith. It was a faith founded upon the knowledge of historic fact, but that knowledge did not alter the Christianity presented. The danger today is that the presentation of Christianity by the neoevangelical with all the intellectual brilliance and excellence may turn out to be a counterfeit version. When the message is reduced to such proportions that the friendship of the world is gained, the approval of Christ is lost, for both cannot be had at the same time.

Fundamentalism has earned much of the criticism which has been given it in this area. Because of the sweeping paralysis which liberalism brought upon the centers of learning, it is understandable why fundamentalism regarded higher learning with an air of suspicion. The pathos of talking down education and the attempt to replace it with "spirituality" must not continue. Spirituality and scholarship need not be antagonists. It must be remembered that neither produces the other. The solution to the problem will not be found in either a sneering at intellectualism or an overemphasis of it.

Carnell sharply accused all fundamentalists of intellectual stagnation. He banded all fundamentalists together and criticized them for rejecting *en toto* all general wisdom and for categorizing everything the unbeliever says as blasphemy. The universality of such accusations hardly savors of intelligence or fairness. Factual evidence presented in a spirit of love—that mark of a true disciple—will not support such condemnatory claims. There must be a proper balance of piety and scholarship. Faith for the child of God need not be blind, but oftentimes it is naked of any intellectual understanding. Whenever any kind or degree of intellectualism "spoils" faith (Col. 2:8), it must be avoided.

Deflection to a Powerless Message

This danger exists because of the strong emphasis on the social aspect and application of the gospel. There is no present warrant to accuse neoevangelicalism of preaching the old social gospel which the liberal preached in the early part of this century. Neoevangelicalism cannot be accused of such a message now because it strongly emphasizes the need of individual regeneration through faith in the atoning work of Christ. ". . . The primary task of the church is to preach Christ, crucified, risen and coming in triumph—the only hope of the individual and of the social order itself."[8]

Neoevangelicalism differs drastically at many other points with the old liberal social gospel. Take, for example, in addition to the need of Christ, the need of the Holy Spirit in salvation. The Bible is also said to be that which leads men to faith in the Son of God as Savior from the guilt and power of sin. These are certainly emphases which set neoevangelicalism's message off as distinct from the liberal social gospel. The failure of the social gospel of modernism is recognized by the neoevangelical. The modernist, it is argued, had "a social passion, devoted to solving these problems but he lacks the supernatural power."[9] Neoevangelicals also realize the errors and inadequacies of the liberal social gospel and do not want to fall into them.

> Modern evangelicalism need not substitute as its primary aim the building of "relatively higher civilizations." To do that is to fall into the error of yesterday's liberalism. Its supreme aim is the proclamation of redeeming grace to sinful humanity; there is no need for Fundamentalism to embrace liberalism's defunct social gospel.[10]

Carl F. H. Henry carefully spelled out the evangelical strategy in his "Perspective for Social Action." In contrast to the social gospel of Protestant liberalism, to which fundamentalism reacted to such an extent that it became socially indifferent, he listed ten aspects of the neoevangelical perspective for social action.

> 1. Christian social leaders *set their cultural objectives in the larger framework of the Christian mission,* and do not regard themselves primarily as social reformers. . . .
> 2. Evangelical social action *throbs with the evangelistic invitation to new life in Jesus Christ.* . . .
> 3. Reliance on the Holy Spirit to sunder the shackles of sin requires *a regard for social evils first in the light of personal wickedness.* . . .
> 4. Evangelicals insist that *social justice is a divine requirement for the whole human race,* not for the Church alone. . . .
> 5. Despite their insistence on the spiritual and moral roots of social evil, evangelicals are aware that *personal sin often finds its occasion in the prevailing community situation.* . . .
> 6. The fellowship within the churches is a mirror of the realities of a new social order. *The new order* is therefore not simply a distant dream; it *exists already in an anticipative way in the regenerate fellowship of the Church.* . . .
> 7. By maintaining the connection between

social reform and the law of love, evangelicals *face the organized evils of society with the power of sanctified compassion. . . .*

8. *The pulpit is to proclaim the revealed will of God, including the ethical principles of the Bible. . . .*

9. *The Christian influence upon society is registered most intimately through family and immediate neighbor relations, and then more broadly in the sphere of vocation* or daily work in which the believer's service of God and man is elaborated in terms of a labor of love, *and then politically as a citizen of two worlds. . . .*

10. *Concern* for righteousness *and justice* throughout the social order *requires the believer as an individual to range himself for or against specific options for social reform and change.*[11]

As they stand, they are both valid and Biblically sound. The danger does not lie in the present perspective, for it is based on the necessity of individual redemption rather than an attempt to foist Christian principles upon a non-Christian society as the liberal social gospel did. The danger lies rather in the possibility of deterioration to what the social gospel became. Obviously, then, the danger in this direction does not lie in what neoevangelicalism now believes but in that which its present emphasis may very well lead it to believe and proclaim.

History is a solemn reminder of the way in which the social gospel movement deteriorated from an individual emphasis and doctrinal basis to a position which was more interested in the masses than the individual and almost entirely neglected doctrine. It is true, no doubt, that the doctrinal basis upon which the social gospel was built was the liberal doctrinal approach, but it was doctrine though it was not in every case orthodox doctrine. The most influential leader of the social gospel movement was Walter Rauschenbusch. His *A Theology for the Social Gospel* gave evidence that the social gospel was not apart from doctrine but aligned with it. The burden of Rauschenbusch was to place the social gospel message in a theological and doctrinal setting.

His constant claim was that the social gospel was not a deviation or detraction from Christian doctrine but an enlargement and intensification of it. He attempted to relate his social gospel message to the traditional orthodox doctrines. The beginnings of the social gospel were traced to the message of Jesus by its proponents. Jesus was interested in meeting the individual physical needs of men. He saw a suffering, poor society and was always willing to heal and help. According to McCown in *The Genesis of the Social Gospel* the early advocates went even beyond the life and message of Jesus for their support. The prophets, it is claimed, proclaimed a personal social message and this message was mirrored in the ministry of Jesus.

Not long after the movement got started, however, it developed into a sickly and weak enthusiasm which was damaged by World War I and shattered by the depression which followed. Change in belief is evident in the ten-year period of 1907 to 1917 in the life of Rauschenbusch himself. Though he still believed in the gradualistic coming of the Kingdom, by 1917 he asserted that its coming would not be by peaceful development only, but by conflict with the kingdom of evil. Clearly then, the Rauschenbusch of 1917 was not the Rauschenbusch of 1907, so far as his doctrine of original sin was concerned. There was a noticeable shift of emphasis in the social gospel movement from individual sin and the need of individual recovery to collective sin and the recovery of society as a whole.

> Interestingly enough the distinctive feature of the social gospel was neither its passion for social justice nor its conviction that Christianity has social relevance. . . . The social gospel knowingly *surrendered* [italics mine] the personal gospel of Jesus Christ's substitutionary death and his supernatural redemption and regeneration of sinful men. . . . The social gospel *became* [italics mine] an *alternative* to the Gospel of supernatural grace and redemption. This divergence became more and more obvious after 1910. Rauschenbusch, who supplied *A Theology for the Social Gospel*

(1917) at the point where the movement had lost spiritual moorings and direction, still propounded the importance of the supernatural regeneration of sinners.[12]

The deterioration evident in the message of the social gospel is also evident in other organizations which are still performing a social service but which have strayed far from their original intent and purpose.

The YMCA is a sad illustration of deflection to a powerless message. Here is an organization which has a rich Christian heritage. The movement began with a vital and Biblical social interest rooted in a gospel of personal redemption. Today this originally evangelical agency has substituted for the gospel a secular and purely social message.[13] The C in the YMCA is confusing. Can this movement still be called Christian?

Two reactions exist to the Christian origin of the movement. Some feel quite proud that the Y could produce men such as George Williams and Dwight L. Moody. In spite of this pride, these men are looked upon as spokesmen for a rather immature type of Christianity. These and other founding fathers and workers are recognized for their zeal to reach the lost but also for their lack of knowledge and acceptance of other religions and interpretations of the faith. Others presently associated with the YMCA react differently, and they are in the minority. They recognize that the organization has strayed from its original basic course. Only a casual observation will reveal how far the movement really has wandered from its original moorings.

The Y was born in evangelism, prayer meetings and Bible study; the educational, social and athletic facilities were added to promote the wholesome life of young men and boys. Contrasting these noble efforts with the efforts of today is very disheartening.

Everet R. Johnson observed the following stumbling blocks to solving the problem of the confusing "Christian" in the YMCA title.

1. The YMCA has reduced Christianity to one of the religions of this world, rather than accepting it as 'truth' and 'fact' from God the Creator. 2. Though we are 'Christian,' we are not biblically-centered. Thus the term 'Christian' has a broad, ineffective, almost nondescript meaning as it is used in our name, the YMCA. 3. Few staff men have convictions on the great doctrines of Christianity, such as the condition of men, Christ's atoning sacrifice, His resurrection, ascension and second coming, and the apocalyptic teachings.[14]

Obviously, what was at the beginning a secondary emphasis for the YMCA— social concern—has now become a major concern to the neglect of the original purpose of introducing young men to Jesus Christ.

A further illustration of a movement which began with high and noble aims grounded in doctrine and individual redemption, but now emblematic of only a social concern, is the Salvation Army. General Booth, the founder, bathed the Army, which was organized in England to minister to the poor and needy, in a strong doctrinal basis. In most of the essentials of the faith the Army aligned itself with the doctrines of the Church of England and of various dissenting Protestant bodies.

Its bedrock is the Bible, especially the New Testament, which it accepts as true without qualification, from the first word to the last, troubling itself with no doubts or criticisms. Especially does it believe in the dual nature of the Saviour, in Christ as God, and in Christ as man, and in the possibility of forgiveness and redemption for even the most degraded and defiled of human beings.[15]

The social work in which the Army was involved was a

. . . mere by-product or consequence of its main idea. Experience has shown that it is of little use to talk about his soul to a man with an empty stomach. . . . The first duty of the Christian is to bind their wounds and soothe their sorrows. After-wards, he may hope to cure them of their

sins, for he knows that unless such a cure is ef-
fected, temporal assistance avails but a little. . . .
The man or woman must be born again, must be
regenerated.[16]

General Booth was a realist. He did not ignore the
Devil as the impulse to evil; neither did he deny the
existence of Hell. He believed profoundly in the power
of the gospel to transform even the most degraded
lives. The Salvation Army originally had a dual
purpose—to win others to Christ and to minister physically to the most degraded of humanity.

One can hardly believe that a movement grounded
so securely in the Bible and interested so sincerely in
the salvation of the individual could move so far from
the faith and interests of its founding father. What was
once a vibrant and pulsating organization for the salvation of men and the securing of their social standing is
now little more than a social reform movement hardly
even operating in a redemptive context.

The social gospel movement, the YMCA and the
Salvation Army are clear examples of what can become
of a movement or organization which begins to major
on minors. The social concern of neoevangelicalism is
not new nor is it wrong. It only becomes wrong when
interest in social sins takes precedence over the need of
individual redemption, when the application of the
message takes priority over the gospel itself.
Neoevangelicalism must think seriously upon this
danger lest what has happened to other organizations,
which began with as doctrinal and individualistic a
basis as neoevangelicalism, will befall it as well. History need not repeat itself, but it oftentimes does, at
least approximately. The very area which the new
evangelicalism is attempting to correct because of the
fundamentalist failure could prove to be the precise
area which will cause the deflection to a powerless message. The trends and directions of the movements discussed above become alarming possibilities "writ
large" for neoevangelicalism.

There is a lot of talk these days about negotiation, especially in the political world. This conversation is not confined to the political world, however; it is becoming more prominent in theological circles, though it is usually not referred to as negotiation. Concessions usually accompany negotiations, and concessions can be very costly. There is always the danger of giving more than the value in turn received. A conciliatory attitude is not to be despised so long as the conciliation produced thereby does not alter the basic underlying beliefs which make the parties involved distinct and unique. When the things which matter most are thrown out, it ceases to be conciliation and becomes accommodation.

In matters of theology it is dangerous for the conservative to concede to the point of accommodation to the nonconservative. When this begins to take place, it is not long until the areas of greatest difference become so foggy that the conservative is hard put to support his belief because he has already accepted too many of the nonconservative's false and unbelieving premises. That this danger exists today in neoevangelicalism is evident from the very nature and purpose of the movement as well as by the admission of some of its proponents and enemies.

In chapter 3 of part III some of the internal fears, unrest and dissatisfactions were presented. These reveal the recognition on the part of neoevangelicals that there is the danger within the movement of being too concessive. In addition to those healthy self-criticisms which have come from within, alarming criticisms are coming from without. Obviously, fundamentalists have reacted differently. Observations have ranged from thoughtful concern and Christian criticism to the pronouncement of the judgment of God upon the men and movement. It is to be expected that fundamentalists will recognize concessions, but even avowed liberals have realized and spoken of some things for which the fundamentalists have been harshly judged by the neoevangelical.

DANGERS IN NEOEVANGELICALISM

The leaders of neoevangelicalism have convinced the liberal that they are attempting to modify certain fundamentalist attitudes and teachings. The liberal sees in neoevangelicalism a sophisticated effort of theological revision. L. Harold DeWolf in his *Present Trends in Christian Thought* sees the following principal revisions of fundamentalist theology in neoevangelicalism:

> 1) There is a noticeable, though indecisive change in the doctrine of biblical inspiration and authority. Some of the new evangelicals, unlike most of the fundamentalists, avoid teaching 'verbal' inspiration of the Bible, stressing rather plenary or full inspiration. This marks a movement to a more flexible position. . . . 2) In regard to the sciences in general, and particularly in relation to the biological theory of evolution, some concessions are being made. The conflict between science and Scripture is played down and some adaptations in interpretation of both are introduced to minimize or eliminate contradictions. . . . 3) Even the stress on sharply defined, exclusive doctrine shows signs of softening. A trend toward greater flexibility has developed largley under the influence of efforts to bring together conservative Calvinists and Arminians, Baptists and Nazarenes, Lutherans and Free Methodists. This requires considerable breadth of dogmatic tolerance.[17]

The second principal revision cited by DeWolf is easily illustrated. Conceding scriptural verities for the speculations of science is a real and existing danger in neoevangelicalism. No doubt, it is the natural result of the other dangers. An unrealistic optimism provides the temptation to neglect a strong doctrinal emphasis. That danger is productive of the desire for intellectual attainment which is often substituted for faith. If and when knowledge takes the place of faith, the danger of applying that philosophy to Scripture in a subjection of it to science is self-evident. And this is precisely what has taken place. Contemporary evangelicalism is seeking to span the chasm which undoubtedly exists between Scripture and science. There is a cleavage between the two, and Scripture represented in orthodox Christianity has suffered most in the conflict. The problem is whether or not orthodoxy is obligated to bring science and Scripture into harmony. Neoevangelicalism is attempting to harmonize the two in as much as that is possible, but in the process Scripture is subjected to science. Some neoevangelicals seem bent on conceding as much as possible to science wherever Scripture is silent or indeterminate.

This existing danger is acknowledged by Henry in his chapter on "Science and Religion" in *Contemporary Evangelical Thought,* a book which he edited:

> Yet certain dangers seem to this writer to attend some recent efforts to bridge the gap between Christianity and science. Such attempts to reconcile Biblical theology and contemporary science frequently run the risk of needless concession. If they do not actually fail to grasp the essential contrast between creation and evolution, they imply, perhaps unwittingly, an acceptance of principles hostile to biblical theism.[18]

This danger of conceding Scripture for the sake of science is seen by Henry to be true in the progressive creationism of Bernard Ramm and the threshold evolution of Edward John Carnell. It would not be fair to accuse Ramm or Carnell of supporting naturalism in the views which they espouse. Ramm with his progressive creation view strongly defended the sovereign and fiat act of creation as a result of the *concept,* plan or purpose which was in the mind of God before creation. He maintained that after the fiat act of creation came the *process* in which God, Who had been working *outside* of nature, turned the task of continuing creation over to the Holy Spirit, Who is *inside* nature.[19]

Carnell challenged the validity of the total evolution scheme in support of his alternative threshold evolution view. His view stated that "there are gaps which exist between the original 'kinds,' while on the 'total' evolution view each 'kind' can be traced back to a more primitive type, and that, to a still more primitive, *ad infinitum*."[20] These original "kinds" "were stock out of which, through threshold evolution, all our present types have evolved."[21]

According to Henry, the problem is not that these views are unorthodox, though they may be questioned.

> The difficulty is that these phrases contribute to a verbal illusion which attracts the interest of the contemporary evolutionist somewhat under false pretenses, and his enthusiasm over their surface impression can only embarrass the evangelical overture. For creation, in its Biblical sense, is something quite distinct from what the scientist insists is "progressively" knit into the warp and woof of reality, which "threshold evolution" can hardly be a part purchase of the developmental rationals if it presumes to be biblical. . . . The employment of conventional phrases with a contrary intention therefore runs needless apologetic hazards.[22]

This must come as a hard saying from one neoevangelical to another, but a clearer statement of the danger cannot be found.

The danger of subjecting Scripture to science is likewise evident in many articles which are appearing in magazines which favor the neoevangelical approach. The discouragement in these articles does not come from their appearance and presentation of the difficulties. Christianity has nothing to hide. Our heads must never be stuck in the sand of unconcern. The problem comes in the failure of these articles to suggest any positive and possible solutions to the problems presented. More questions and problems are raised than are solved. The overtone of many of them is that maybe the orthodox cannot be as sure of their Biblical beliefs as they once were. Maybe science is right and Scripture is wrong after all.

Carnell in *The Case for Orthodox Theology* was guilty of this very concession. He spoke of manifesting Christian love toward those holding to a number of authors of Isaiah. He was altogether too friendly to evolution, and he suggested that no principle would be forfeited if orthodoxy surrendered the immediate creation theory out of respect for paleontology (the branch of geology which studies life as shown by fossil or stonelike remains of animals and plants), as it surrendered the literal-day theory out of respect for geology (the science which investigates the structure of the earth and its successive physical changes).[23] One wonders where this subjection will stop. Such neoevangelical approaches to the differences between Scripture and science have actually caused Scripture, and those who believe it to be divinely authoritative in all its pronouncements, more disrepute by these compromising endeavors.

Joseph T. Bayly in his review of Ramm's *The Christian View of Science and Scriptures* questioned Ramm's interpretation of the flood in Genesis 6. Ramm believed the flood described was merely a local event. He believed this though he admitted that his view may not agree with the Biblical language description.

> At this point, although the author claims that inspiration is not involved—only interpretation—we have met one of the basic problems which could conceivably change evangelical Christianity's view of Scripture and inspiration. If the Biblical narrator presented an erroneous view of the flood's universality in language which convinced readers that mankind was destroyed until modern geology showed that it was merely local, can we any longer honestly claim to believe that divine inspiration has protected the whole Bible from error?[24]

Bayly further expressed dissatisfaction with Ramm's presentation in the same book of the Fall and the chapters in Genesis which present it. Ramm quoted at some length from J. S. Whale, who discredited the

tific statement or happening. The tragedy in Ramm's
presentation of Whale's unbelief is that he did not
comment on it. The same is true of his quotation from
Alan Richardson, which includes the following statement: "Hence these chapters [Genesis 1-11] have an
existential not scientific character."[25] One would expect
Ramm to comment and give his opinion on these rash
quotations; otherwise, the reader is left in doubt as to
whether he accepts or rejects these conclusions.

John W. Sanderson, Jr. joined in legitmately
criticizing the extreme concessions of neoevangelicalism.

> (1) Neoevangelicals, so anxious to carry on conver-
> sations with Liberals, are in danger of absorbing
> Liberalism's attitudes, at the cost of losing the
> sharp edge of Evangelicalism's basic beliefs. (2)
> Even if these men, whose orthodoxy is un-
> doubted, do not themselves succumb to unbelief,
> they have set an example which their disciples will
> follow directly into rejection of the Scripture. (3) In
> their desire to change the direction of Fundamen-
> talism, the Neo-Evangelicals have not exhibited
> care in Scriptural exegesis and in handling histori-
> cal data. The Fundamentalist counterattack seems
> to be saying that Neo-Evangelicals are in danger of
> committing the sin Dr. Carnell imputes to
> Fundamentalism—"to appear better by making
> the others worse."[26]

Certainly, these timely warnings ought not to go
unheeded, especially since many of them come from
within the framework of those who recognize the failures of fundamentalism but are not willing to forsake
the bedrock upon which fundamentalism is built. It is
not merely a matter of words. Words take on new
meanings and carry varied overtones. It is rather a matter of what the words mean to the hearer and how he
reacts when they are used. May God spare the
neoevangelicals, in their desire to communicate to the
nonconservative, from conceding to the point of losing
that firm belief in things which matter most.

Perhaps the cost of conceding significant areas is already beginning to make itself known. This came with real force when Reinhold Niebuhr said after several encounters with Carnell relative to his neoorthodoxy that Carnell "agrees with me up to the point of verifying the Christian faith in the experience of redemption."[27] Evidently Carnell did not succeed in his communication with Niebuhr because in his mind the area of greatest difference between them was given away by Carnell.

The neoevangelical needs to be reminded that in order to establish a meaningful rapprochement with liberalism and neoorthodoxy he must concede to these groups his orthodox interpretation of those very vital areas which make him distinct from them. To give away these things which make the difference between conservatism and nonconservatism is obviously more costly than the evangelical can afford since it would remove any reason for his existence as an evangelical.

The liberal may look at these concessions as indicative of progress and theological evolutionary betterment for the evangelical cause, but the alert conservative cannot evaluate them in the same way. For the conservative such concessions, if persisted in, will be detrimental and will cause irreparable damage to the cause of Christ. Many have recognized the seriousness of these concessions and are offering constructive criticism. The self-criticism and the criticism from those without are among the most healthy signs of stemming the tide of concessions.

Amalgamation with Unbelief

Alignment with evil systems and avowed enemies has never profited the church. History reveals that any attempt of such association has always brought disrepute upon the cause of Christ. The demands of the enemies of the cross are too high and costly for the church. Christianity must be de-Christianized to gain favor with its foes.

In the second century the apologists attempted to

give Christianity a place in the empire. In order to accomplish this aim they couched Christianity in the philosophical terminology of their day. They attempted a most dangerous harmony between the revelation of God and the pagan philosophies. For them, Christianity became the highest type of philosophy attested to by revelation. Thus, in order to make Christianity comprehensible they forced it into a foreign framework. The result of their work was that the Biblical doctrines soon lost their real meanings because of the abstract philosophical terms which were used to explain them.

The attempt of the scholastics of the Middle Ages was to prove the reasonableness of the church's doctrines in a rapidly changing society. Was not this a vital factor which made necessary the Reformation? The church would have been far wiser to rely on the Bible than to attempt an amalgamation with the shifting views of science and philosophy. When theology became the handmaiden of philosophy instead of philosophy being the handmaiden of theology, the church lost its power in the world.

The church has been commissioned with a twofold responsibility for every age—the preservation and propagation of the faith. There is hardly a supremacy of one of these duties over the other, but there is an order of priority in the discharging of the responsibility. Obviously, if the faith is not preserved, it cannot be propagated. Whenever the church, or any segment of it, elevates the propagation of its message, at any cost, to the neglect of the preservation of its message, it is defeating its very purpose for existence. It is then no longer a light penetrating the darkness but has become part of the darkness.

For many this amalgamation with unbelief is a great danger in neoevangelicalism. The fact of the neoevangelical's association with unbelief in the areas of theology and science is very evident. The danger arises out of the fact that the communication and cooperation which neoevangelicalism seeks to promote may lead to an amalgamation with the very unbelief which it is attempting to affect.

The association with unbelief in the area of theology is observable in the desire for an exchange of ideas with liberalism. This desire, of course, comes from a weak view of scriptural separation. Earlier it was pointed out that neoevangelicals neglect the doctrine of separation. Here it is only necessary to be reminded of the accompanying danger of such a neglect. Separation in the minds of neoevangelicals prohibits the interchange of viewpoints with the liberal and neoorthodox. It is felt that such prohibitions make it impossible to present orthodoxy as a live option for a world view. Therefore, the neoevangelical is desirous of an opportunity to exchange theological table talk with nonevangelicals. The believer, it is emphasized, is obligated to remain in the communion that gave him spiritual birth, regardless of the associations with unbelief which that church may have, so long as the creedal statements remain untampered. Neoevangelicalism finds no Biblical warrant for ecclesiastical separation.

Others call for the avoidance of the modernist-fundamentalist debate for practical reasons.

> Because of the modern premium on ecclesiastical unity, because of the inelegant impression church controversy makes upon the world, because of the easy degeneration of theological conflict into negation and lovelessness, and because of the rising generation of churchgoers who must be linked swiftly with the first generation of Christian faith, there is a growing impatience today with the effort to preserve the edge of the past generation's theological debate as the permanent center of Christian polemics, apologetics, and evangelism.[28]

A two-fold difficulty is attached to the neoevangelical view of ecclesiastical separation. In the first place, it is not consistent with the claim to proclaim the whole counsel of God. Certainly, Paul called for a separation between believers because of immorality and disobedience to the Scriptures (1 Cor. 5; 2 Thess. 3). Then, too, the same writer begs the brethren to "mark them which cause divisions and offences contrary to the doctrine which ye have learned; and avoid them" (Rom. 16:17). The reason for the avoidance follows: "For they that are such serve not our Lord Jesus Christ, but their own belly; and by good words and fair speeches deceive the hearts of the simple" (Rom. 16:18). Quite clearly, then, the Roman believers were to avoid those who caused divisions and offenses contrary to sound doctrine for two reasons: they serve not our Lord Jesus Christ and they deceive the hearts of the simple. It is difficult to understand the rejection of such explicit teaching especially when it is contained in the Book of Romans, for it is claimed dogmatically that "Romans and Galatians are the highest ranking sources in theology. . . ."[29]

Secondly, the neoevangelical view of ecclesiastical separation is not consistent with the clear teaching of 1 Corinthians 2 and 3. The natural man is one who is unable to discern spiritual truth because he does not possess the spiritual life; he is dead spiritually. Neoevangelicals are often attempting to learn spiritual truth and to share spiritual understanding with those who are dead spiritually and unable to contribute to any spiritual knowledge. This does not mean that the liberal and neoorthodox cannot teach the evangelical anything. Usually they are more informed in many areas of secular learning than the evangelical. It does mean, however, that the unregenerate cannot teach the regenerate any spiritual truth, for to the natural man God's truth is foolishness.

In the area of science the danger of amalgamation with unbelief is evident from the attempts to harmonize Scripture with the findings of science. Concessions in this area were revealed earlier; now it is necessary to reveal the danger of such concessions. The Word of God must always be clearly defensible before every attack of unbelief, but this is not to imply that God's truth must bow at the theories of man. When the Scripture is accommodated to satisfy the speculation of man, there is little hope that man will be able to maintain belief in it.

Perhaps the believer needs to be reminded that the theory of evolution, for example, is only the best which the unbelieving heart and mind can produce since the Word of God has been rejected. The unbelievers are becoming increasingly aware of the sharp antithesis between Christianity and its opponents, and it is time that the believer reaffirm his belief in the same. Great advances have been made for Christianity in recent years, but maybe some of those advances have been made at the cost of Christianity itself.

To summarize this danger, it may be said that its seriousness lies in the close proximity with which the new evangelicalism seeks to cooperate with unbelief. The effects of such cooperation may not be realized immediately, but if history is a criterion upon which to base judgment, the effects will come. The danger is that the neoevangelical brethren will become so closely associated with unbelief that they will move beyond the point of no return. Many fear that they will be so enamored with the desire to propagate the faith that they will concede to the point of losing the faith and will be absorbed in the unbelief from which God has delivered them.

Should the trends and dangers discussed in this chapter develop to their possible extent, they would eventuate in the destruction of that which is at the very heart of orthodoxy. The new evangelicalism would then cease to be either *new* or *evangelical.* It would not be new because other movements which began essentially on the same basis have deteriorated into approaches which are not worthy of the name Christian. It would not be evangelical because the realization of the dangers referred to would place the movement completely outside that which has Biblically and traditionally been called evangelical. A hope which is shared by many is

that these existing dangers will never eventuate in the
reductions which seem inevitable at the present time
from the prospect of history and present circumstances.
Neoevangelicalism itself must answer the imperative
question: "Which is more important, purity of testimony or opportunity?"[30]

NOTES

1. Henry, *Evangelical Responsibility*, p. 55.

2. Ibid., pp. 50, 51.

3. Carl F. H. Henry, "What's Next?" *Eternity* (January 1970);
James Sire, "Futurology," *Eternity* (January 1977); "Learn More
About Tomorrow," *Christian Life* (May 1974); Vernon C. Grounds,
"Premillennial and Social Pessimism," *Christian Heritage* (October
1974); "The Thrust of the Seventies," *Eternity* (January 1970).

4. Christopher Driver, "The Idea of a Christian University,"
Frontier (June 1970).

5. "Evangelicals and Fundamentals," *Christianity Today* (September 16, 1957), p. 21.

6. Carnell, *The Case for Orthodox Theology*, pp. 121, 128.

7. James Orr, *The Progress of Dogma* (Grand Rapids: Wm. B.
Eerdmans Publishing Co., 1960), p. 178.

8. Carl F. H. Henry, "Evangelicalism and the New Birth,"
Christianity Today (July 7, 1958), p. 23.

9. Harold J. Ockenga, "Evangelical Emphasis," *Bulletin of Fuller Theological Seminary* (July—September 1953), pp. 2, 4.

10. Henry, *The Uneasy Conscience. . . ,* p. 10.

11. Henry, "Perspective for Social Action."

12. Ibid.

13. "Will the 'Y' Recover Its Gospel?" *Christianity Today*
(November 11, 1957).

14. Everet R. Johnson, "The Confusing 'C' in YMCA," *Christianity Today* (April 14, 1958), p. 7.

15. Henry Rider Haggard, *Regeneration* (London: Longmans,
Green and Co., 1910), p. 229.

16. Ibid., p. 234.

17. DeWolf, *Present Trends in Christian Thought*, pp. 44-47.

18. Carl F. H. Henry, "Science and Religion," *Contemporary
Evangelical Thought*, p. 116.

19. Ramm, *The Christian View of Science and Scripture*, p. 116.

20. Edward J. Carnell, *An Introduction to Christian Apologetics*
(Grand Rapids: Wm. B. Eerdmans Publishing Co., 1948), p. 239.

21. Ibid., footnote 24, p. 242.

22. Henry, *Contemporary Evangelical Thought*, pp. 250-252.

23. Carnell, *The Case for Orthodox Theology*, pp. 95, 98.

24. Joseph T. Bayly, review of *The Christian View of Science and
Scripture* by Bernard Ramm, *Eternity* (August 1955), p. 47.

25. Ibid.

26. John W. Sanderson, "Neo-Evangelicalism and Its Critics," *The Sunday School Times* (January 28, 1961), p. 82.

27. "The Library of Living Theology," II, 443, cited by *The Sunday School Times* (February 4, 1961), p. 90.

28. Henry, *Evangelical Responsibility*, p. 17.

29. Carnell, *The Case for Orthodox Theology*, p. 66.

30. John W. Sanderson, "Purity of Testimony—or Opportunity," *The Sunday School Times* (February 11, 1961), p. 110.

2

Dangers for the Fundamentalist

FUNDAMENTALISM is a twentieth-century expression of Biblical Christianity. It has not always been an accurate and valid expression. Perhaps the gravest peril for fundamentalists is the assumption that they alone possess the truth. Sometimes one's interpretation of truth is identified as the truth and hence all who differ are considered to be in error. No movement is beyond reproach. It is sheer folly to assume that anyone or any movement has arrived at the place beyond which progress can be made.

Fundamentalism is basically and fundamentally a theological and doctrinal position, but since its beginning it has inherited groups who claim shelter in the name but have done the cause serious harm. In other words, there are fundamentalists and then there are fundamentalists. The honest fundamentalist will humbly admit that the message and witness of fundamentalism has had its black strands. He will use the failures of the past to guide him to success in the future.

> Its witness may have been truncated, or even perverse in spots (let him who is without sin cast the first stone), but it fought a battle against impressive odds when almost every scholarly citadel of

157

the faith capitulated. Indeed, the critic of Fundamentalism today can thank his God that someone fought for the most important doctrines of the
faith.[1]

Some of the unessential accretions of fundamentalism have earned disrepute for the whole movement.
This is lamentable and regrettable but nevertheless
true. Contemporary fundamentalism is at the cross-
roads, and the choice it makes will determine its success or failure. This is an unprecedented opportunity to
utilize the criticisms even though some of them have
been unjust and have been given in an un-Christian
manner. The criticisms can be used to good advantage
if the fundamentalists will acknowledge failure, build
on the past and continue to proclaim the unsearchable
riches of Christ. Should fundamentalism fail to do this
and instead resort to pride, highmindedness, back-
biting, bickering and fighting among the brethren and
thereby proclaim a powerless and lifeless message, it
will have failed God and man in the most crucial and
strategic hour of its existence.

The dangers, therefore, for fundamentalism do not
lie in the hard core of doctrinal essentials which make it
distinct but in the way in which those doctrinal essentials have been, and sometimes still are, presented and
in the way its adherents react to criticism and opposition. The answer to the perplexing situation in conservatism is not to be found in the battle over terms,
neither in a discarding and soft-pedaling of the essentials but in the discarding of attitudes and actions
which are contrary to true Christian character and a
return to the proclamation of the "thus saith the Lord"
and "the whole counsel of God"—not in mere lip service but with all integrity and boldness.

The dangers which follow will no doubt be read
with varying reactions by fundamentalists. The writer
is not intending to speak for fundamentalism. These
are merely dangers as he sees them. They are presented
prayerfully and seriously but without apology, for they

Universal Condemnations

It is valid to criticize neoevangelicalism for group-
ing all fundamentalists together in their condemnations. Often neoevangelicals fail to distinguish between the good and the bad in fundamentalism. They
"throw out the baby with the bath," as one writer put
it. Yet, this is precisely the sin of which the fundamentalist is too often guilty. One of the first things which
must be learned in this connection is that there is a
great breadth of latitude in belief among neoevangelicals as there is among fundamentalists. Men cannot be
categorically received or condemned just because they
have been in some way or another identified with a
movement. This is as true in neoevangelicalism as it is
in fundamentalism. For the most part, neoevangelicals
have sincere desires and give evidence of pure motives.
They want to communicate with the nonconservatives.
They want to present evangelicalism as a world view
which can be intelligently presented, understood and
defended. They do not intend to cause division
and disunity in the Body of Christ. The fundamentalist who
does not distinguish men from movements is exhibiting an attitude which is contrary to that which Christ
displayed. With all of His denunciation of the Pharisees
as a group He was delighted to take time to show
Nicodemus, a ruler among them, the way of life.

The danger of this universal condemnation not
only operates in the area of men within the movement
but also in relation to various views which the men
hold. Everything a man says or contributes must not be
rejected because of disagreement on a specific thing.
Though disagreement is valid, it should not result in
blanket denunciations of all which the man believes.
This kind of activity only antagonizes and does nothing
to heal the breach but rather needlessly widens it. For
example, a man's view of the method by which the
gospel is to be applied to society may be wrong, but it

does not necessarily follow that he has a false gospel. Each individual and each doctrine must be evaluated separately. This is especially true of those in neoevangelicalism. It is dangerous to condemn because of association and without examination. The friends of the Lord would have had many opportunities to condemn Him because of His association. He ate with publicans and sinners and conversed at length with an adulterous woman, to cite but two examples.

Association alone is not a valid criterion for the pronouncement of guilt upon an individual. It is too easy to be associated without an entire commitment either with a movement's strengths or weaknesses. In neoevangelicalism and fundamentalism one can be orthodox in doctrine and heterodox in practice. This evidently was the problem of the religious leaders of Christ's day. He denounced them not because they subscribed to false doctrine but because they were self-righteous, unloving and proud. The need exists for both fundamentalists and neoevangelicals to so live that their Lord will not need to rebuke them either for false belief or false practice regardless of the label under which they minister.

The existence and continuance of wholesale condemnations of all neoevangelicals because of the failures and extremities of some is indicative of one of two things. This attitude reveals either a lack of information or a lack of integrity to present the facts honestly, or both. Strangely enough, some who minister under the label of neoevangelicalism are offering more intelligent and objective criticisms of the movement than are many who minister under the label of fundamentalism. Many neoevangelicals are equally as unhappy with the accretions which neoevangelicalism has already gained as are fundamentalists with some of the fanatics who parade under the banner of fundamentalism. In light of these facts it is unsound to ascribe universal condemnations or praises of all who are associated with either neoevangelicalism or fundamentalism.

The sharp disagreements which exist between fundamentalists and neoevangelicals often cause fundamentalists to refuse to be informed firsthand of neoevangelical developments. Pet phrases and clichés which exhibit either isolated or outmoded ideas but do not demonstrate an understanding of their meanings are often used. Too often an area of disagreement is discovered and stressed out of proportion to areas of agreement. Or one man associated with the movement who is an extremist is paraded as representative of the entire movement without any consideration of change, development or deviation.

Fundamentalists, in order to adequately appraise neoevangelicalism, must keep abreast of the changes and developments in the contemporary scene. They cannot afford to level criticisms on the basis of statements which were made five or ten years ago unless those statements can be substantiated in the present scene. Neoevangelicalism, represented by some of its leaders, has shifted from its original extremely friendly attitude toward nonconservatives and bitter assaults of fundamentalism to a more cautious attitude in its appraisal of both of these movements. On the other hand, other leaders representing neoevangelicalism have become more friendly toward the foe and more pugnacious toward fundamentalism. Fundamentalists must be informed of these shifts in attitude.

Hasty and undocumented statements and generalizations serve only to misinform and bring ridicule upon the fundamentalist. It appears at times as though some fundamentalists break all speed limits in order to be the first to publish their views without any respect for ethics and honesty. Such periodic blunders do a great deal more harm than good. Injustices are often done not only to brethren who minister in different circles but also to the fundamentalist constituency because of haste and lack of sufficient information. It is a responsibility of the believer to preserve and defend the faith against every foe, but it is also his duty to discharge that responsibility accurately and with Christian courtesy.

Unfortunate and incorrect statements give added reason for the neoevangelical to criticize fundamentalism of being a cultic temperament and a mood rather than a theology. Inaccurate statements and generalizations only perpetuate the cleavage. Not only is it necessary to be informed of present developments, but it is also necessary to get more than one man's view before assigning that view to everyone in the movement. It must be remembered, as was indicated earlier, neoevangelicals differ among themselves on some of the essentials.

In addition to the danger of being uninformed, there is also the danger of being ill-advised. In other words, one may be informed but may be informed wrongly. Secondhand source material is often used in evaluations of the new evangelicalism. Someone reads an original source and prints an article in a magazine concerning neoevangelicalism. Perhaps, and this is frequently the case, the original source was misinterpreted and misunderstood and not always knowingly or intentionally. But, nevertheless, scores of others read the article, quote from it, and perhaps even reprint it without consulting any original sources and thus the error is perpetuated. For an accurate and valid critique of neoevangelicalism, fundamentalists must be conversant with the writings of the neoevangelicals, not merely with what some other fundamentalist said or wrote about them.

Then, too, the danger exists of taking statements out of context to prove a point. This also gives a wrong impression and advises people falsely. No doubt the sincere desire of the fundamentalist to sound warnings and issue defenses for the faith provides him with this temptation, but that is no excuse for indulgence in the sin. Not infrequently, articles appear in publications treating neoevangelicalism quite extensively with very brief quotations from writings of neoevangelicals from which dogmatic conclusions are drawn quite apart from the context in which those quotations originally appeared.

The mistakes to which the reader has been alerted in this section are not characteristic of all fundamentalists. They are true, however, of a sufficiently large number to bring disrepute upon a very noble and God-honoring cause.

The best way to be informed and advised properly of neoevangelicalism is to be acquainted with publications which claim to represent the movement. *Christianity Today,* a magazine published fortnightly, is an official representation for the new evangelicalism. *Eternity* and *United Evangelical Action* are others which treat neoevangelicalism favorably. Also, neoevangelicals are publishing books which express their doctrinal and practical viewpoints. Names of these can be secured by observing the footnotes in this book. Books and magazines which objectively criticize neoevangelicalism should also be read and studied along with the writings which favor it. The Fall 1960 issue of the *Central Conservative Baptist Quarterly* contained a bibliography on the new evangelicalism which was quite complete at the time of its compilation and serves as a guide for those interested in further study of the subject. The bibliography contained materials favorable and unfavorable to the new evangelicalism. Also a selective, updated bibliography appears at the back of this book.

Failing To Stand for the Truth Graciously

This danger will be present as long as fundamentalism seeks to defend the faith. There will always be the temptation, inspired of Satan himself, to despise the sinner because of his sin. This is true of everyone, not only the fundamentalist, and must be constantly guarded against in contending for the faith. Those who are faithful in discharging their responsibility to preserve the faith must always speak the truth in love

(Eph. 4:15). The Word of God makes no distinction in the ways in which the truth is to be proclaimed to friend or foe. The truth must always be proclaimed and preserved in love. Evidence of love in these areas will be manifested in the spirit which is displayed. Love is hard to hide and so is hate.

If the truth is to be defended graciously and in love before the unbelieving and those who have turned aside from sound doctrine, then certainly the same is true when believers are in view. The truth of the matter is if love out of a pure heart is not displayed, the charge to defend the faith has not been completely obeyed (1 Tim. 1:5). This exercise of love and graciousness does not mean the defense becomes less forceful; it does mean that it will keep the heart from becoming bitter toward the brethren. Paul exhorts that "all bitterness, and wrath, and anger, and clamour, and evil speaking, be put away" (Eph. 4:31). These things must be put away because they not only hinder the defense of the faith but they also hinder the spiritual lives of the persons who display them and those affected by them. Was not this danger of bitterness the burden and warning on the heart of the writer of the Hebrews? "Looking diligently lest any man fail of the grace of God; lest any root of bitterness springing up trouble you, and thereby many be defiled" (Heb. 12:15).

The seriousness of a gradual deflection from the faith has caused some ungracious and fleshly attitudes to prevail among those with differing convictions. These failures must not be perpetuated. Warnings must continue to go forth and the faith must continually be contended for, but these responsibilities must not be discharged in a contentious spirit. Both neoevangelicals and fundamentalists need to be reminded that the Paul who wrote, "And have no fellowship with the unfruitful works of darkness, but rather reprove them" (Eph. 5:11) is the Paul who wrote the great treatise on love (1 Cor. 13). The John who wrote, "If there come any unto you, and bring not this doctrine, receive him not into your house, neither bid him God speed" (2 John 10) is the John who wrote, "This is my commandment, That ye love one another, as I have loved you" (John 15:12). We need balance in these things and a recognition of the unity in the Body of Christ. The baptism into the Body of Christ does not remove distinctions and differences which exist among the members, but it does reveal the necessity of *every* member. No member can rid himself of the others, for all are needed to complete the Body; we are members one of another.

NOTE

1. John W. Sanderson, "Fundamentalism and Its Critics," *The Sunday School Times* (January 21, 1961), p. 66.

3

Summary

THIS BOOK WILL have served its purpose well if the reader has been made aware of the true essence of neoevangelicalism. In an impersonal way and without bitterness we have surveyed the developments, doctrines, difficulties and dangers of neoevangelicalism. The paths into which this plan has led us have not all been easy. It is hoped that none of them has led the reader into nonessentials but rather has made him cognizant of the vital issues involved in this subject.

The history of the church is replete with evidences of defenses of the faith. The church has always had to define the essence of Christianity. Tests of orthodoxy are not new. Any attempt to minimize or narrow the test is not only to disobey the injunction of Scripture but also to break with the scriptural traditions of our fathers. Opposition and heresy from without and within have made defense of the faith always an imperative. Oftentimes the defense took the form of severe polemics. Take, for example, the written apologies of the second century when scholarly men such as Justin Martyr and Tertullian, seeking to defend orthodox Christianity against its severest opponents, addressed emperors. Then think of the Reformation when men such as Luther, Calvin and Knox defended the faith, especially the soteriological aspect, in unerring fashion. Also, in the early days of the twentieth century, when liberalism was taking its toll, men such as James Orr, J. Gresham Machen and others came to the defense of historic Christianity. However much these men may be criticized, it must be admitted that they accomplished their tasks in an admirable fashion.

Our day is similar to theirs. The battle for truth must ever be fought until He Who is the Personification of truth shall come and put down forever all opposition to Himself and His people. Until that day comes, His message and those who truly proclaim it will be despised by the unbeliever. Every effort to be true to Him must constantly be evaluated and open to new ways to present the old gospel.

This study has revealed the fact that there is a desire to forsake the term *fundamentalism* because of some of the people and problems associated with it. This is hardly justifiable since the term *evangelicalism,* which is to take its place, is also open to new meanings because the liberal often claims to be evangelical. An unbiased criticism against those who judge fundamentalism unjustly is given by William Hordern: "We must remember however, that fundamentalism as a system can no more be justly judged by what its fanatics do than America can be justly judged by what every irresponsible tourist does."[1]

Perhaps we have been deceived into thinking that the failures of fundamentalism (and there have been many) are the sole cause for the rejection of the Christian message by the enemies of the cross. The basic reason for the rejection of Christianity is not its failures but Christianity itself. The attempt to change the emphasis and remove the stigma by changing the label tends to open the door for new meanings which are not precise and clear-cut and which may not at all have been intended. While this present day is unique in many ways, this world is still not a friend of grace. *Fundamentalism* is a term which is quite generally understood today as altogether distinct from liberalism. Why change the name to neoevangelicalism? Why not simply repent of the failures of fundamentalism and retain its fortunes?

This is a day of change. Nobody wants to be out-of-date or old-fashioned. Advances in secular learning are taking men's minds away from the Bible and sometimes turning them against it. Bible scholars are being called upon to discard much of the theological jargon of former days; they are obligated to restate the truths of God understandingly for the atomic age. "But such a day as this is not without its dangers; after clearing away the ramshackle structures of erroneous interpretation, we must be careful in building our new structure that we do not shift our foundation from the rock beneath."[2] That rock is the living and written Word of God. After all the restating of Christianity is completed and if the Biblical moorings are lost, the church will be producing philanthropists, not saints. The church will hum with social activity but will not be composed of holy men. The social application of the gospel must not be disparaged, but neither must it be allowed to take precedence over the gospel itself. The words which Mahatma Gandhi is reputed to have said to an English missionary are fitting at this point: "The great difficulty with Westerners is that they start doing before being."

Neoevangelicalism accuses fundamentalism of having lost the social passion; yet the great peril of neoevangelicalism is to make social interest the center and the gospel message the circumference considered in light of it. Social injustices and abuses abounded when Christ was here; but He did not seek social reform; neither did He give any marching orders to His Church to correct social ills or to purify the existing government. He did commission them, though, with a message and a power which could transform the individual and which turned the world upside down.

That a cleavage exists between neoevangelicalism and fundamentalism is no secret. That cleavage will not be healed by ignoring it or by minimizing the differences. Neither will it be healed by continuing the warfare among the brethren. Sins have been committed on both sides, and new attempts must be made if orthodoxy is to be effective. Both sides must take account of their assets and liabilities. Self-criticism will bring mutual confession and understanding.

Three positive steps can be taken in an effort to heal the breach between neoevangelicalism and fundamentalism and to present a united testimony for Christ. *First,* both need to repent of past failures and do some housecleaning. Fundamentalism needs to confess that elements of its constituency have not always presented its message of truth in love. While the message is right, the method of proclaiming and defending it has not always exhibited Christian grace and courtesy. Neoevangelicalism, too, must confess that some of its leaders are making concessions which could destroy the very heart of evangelicalism. Bitterness and harshness toward brethren who differ can be found in their literature too. If they are honest, they will acknowledge that there has been an overemphasis on the social aspect of the gospel to the neglect of other truth.

Second, both need to recognize the perils in their movements. The peril of generalization has been introduced in both approaches. Ascribing the views of a few to all in the movement has been the fault of fundamentalists and neoevangelicals alike. Guilt by association is a possible danger which must be realized whenever any label is used. Each individual must decide with whom he prefers to be classified. The peril of compromising with unbelief must likewise be recognized and reckoned with by neoevangelicals. Fellowship and cooperation with those who have a broad and uncertain foundation can only result in the dilution and neutralization of the true gospel message. It may not be completely realized in this generation, but drifting in the sand of uncertainty has already begun and who knows what the devastating outcome may be in future generations. Neoevangelicalism must remember its responsibility to future generations. Maybe some have forgotten that the only reason conservative Protestantism is virile and effective today is because our forefathers defended and proclaimed it so polemically.

Third, both fundamentalism and neoevangelicalism must return to a renewed proclamation of the Word in its totality. Both sides give the implication that there is a Biblical antithesis between a strong doctrinal stand and the exercise of Christian responsibilities and ethics. Neoevangelicalism apparently sees social passion as the crying need of the hour, while fundamentalism views the defense of the faith as the most important task. Both of these emphases are necessary and Biblical; however, the one quite obviously takes precedence over the other, for if the faith is not preserved, it cannot be applied to the needs of the world. Is it possible that neoevangelicalism and fundamentalism are stressing their individual points of emphases so much that while they intend to proclaim the entire Word, they are only proclaiming part of it? Perhaps the attention of both groups has been diverted, not to messages which are foreign to the Bible but to messages which are incomplete in that they do not encompass all of the Bible. Neoevangelicalism and fundamentalism must stop preaching merely about the Bible and again start preaching the Bible. When the whole counsel of God is obeyed and proclaimed, balance is achieved between what one believes and how he acts.

* * * * * *

Since the original preparation of this material, additional significant and serious developments have become noticeable among neoevangelicals. One of the emphases throughout this work has been upon the dangers inherent in the new evangelical approach. These dangers are being heightened by the increased concessions which are being made for the sake of unity and compatibility.

In addition to the increased doctrinal concessions, there is a considerable rise in the spread of neo-evangelicalism as it is being espoused by many in responsible places of leadership. This is true especially in educational institutions. A growing number of schools that have been known in the past for their stand with fundamentalism now have men on their faculties who speak very highly of neoevangelicalism and teach its principles to the students. The results have been and will continue to be devastating, not only because the students are confused, but also because the Bible is being de-emphasized. Young men who felt called to the ministry are being encouraged to major in everything else but the Bible. For many of these professors neo-evangelicalism provides a long-desired release from some of the stigmas attached to fundamentalism.

An equally serious development is to be seen in the increased disrepute being brought upon fundamentalism and fundamentalists. The more charitable the neoevangelical becomes to the liberal and neoorthodox the less charitable he becomes to the fundamentalist. The more the neoevangelical appreciates the "advances" of the nonconservatives and their "return to Biblical theology" the more he fails to appreciate and thank God for the noble way in which fundamentalism has preserved the truth of God from the attacks of the enemy. The faults and extremes of cults which minister under the name of fundamentalism have been attributed to the main stream of fundamentalism. This is indeed paradoxical since the fringe elements of fundamentalism, from which most of the neoevangelical criticism comes, are welcomed for the sake of unity into the National Association of Evangelicals while in many cases the mainstream of fundamentalism has not accepted its fringe elements. In the midst of all the criticisms of fundamentalism there is a stupendous neglect to appreciate its faithfulness to the Word of God and contributions to the cause of Christ.

* * * * * *

C. Stacey Woods, once associated with *The Sunday School Times,* wrote an article entitled "The Neutral Protestants." Since the concluding remarks of his article express so well my own sentiments, I would like them to serve as my own conclusion to this section.

If American Protestantism is to survive as a force in this nation, it will not survive in an atmosphere of indeterminate syncretism and latitudinarian ecumenicity that would say that we insist too much upon the importance of doctrine; that the main thing is that we continue the dialogue and get together and understand one another.

Rather American Protestantism will survive when Christians will not shrink from being called narrow and obscurantists, when the only acceptance they desire or the only approval they seek is the acceptance and approval of God, when, like Luther of old, they can say, "Here I stand," and when, like Wesley of old, they can sing triumphantly:

Jesus the prisoner's fetters breaks,
    And bruises Satan's head;
Power into strengthless souls he speaks,
    And life into the dead.

His only righteousness I show,
    His saving truth proclaim;
'Tis all my business here below,
    To cry, "Behold the Lamb!"

Happy, if with my latest breath
    I may but gasp his name;
Preach him to all, and cry in death,
    "Behold, behold the Lamb!"[3]

NOTES

1. Hordern, *A Layman's Guide to Protestant Theology,* pp. 69, 70.

2. C. Stacey Woods, "The Neutral Protestants," *Evangelical Action* (February 1961).

3. Ibid.

Part V

FURTHER DEVELOPMENTS

1

The Basic Conflict

THERE IS A revolution going on inside evangelicalism! It is a revolution of profound proportion with catastrophic consequences sure to follow.

I wish the facts recorded in this chapter would not be true. It is not with glee or the "I-told-you-so" attitude that I write the update of this book, first published in 1959. In the several reprintings since that time, I have provided minor additions to help keep the book current. A number of significant developments since the last edition make this new edition imperative. Neoevangelicals have not been able to hold the line (see pp. 120-125). Two books are of special importance in this connection: *The Young Evangelicals* and *The Worldly Evangelicals*, both by Richard Quebedeaux.

The year 1976 may have been called "the year of the evangelical" as the result of the Gallup Poll, but the fold is more divided than ever before. Nearly fifty million Americans may claim to be born again, but the ranks are riddled with departure from and denial of the historic orthodox view of the Bible.

When neoevangelicalism was born in the forties, it strongly reacted to what its spokesmen called the "dis-

tasteful cultural and social elements of fundamentalism." Fundamentalists were said to have too little
fun, too much damn, and not enough mental. They
were accused of fighting too much and loving too little.
The early pioneers of the new evangelical mentality
said the fundamentalist-modernist battle was over and
insisted that on the denominational and organizational
level, the modernist or liberal had won. Neoevangelicals proposed at that time to present a unified, positive
approach to the world, "to renew the spirit of the New
Testament and the primitive church in the secular age."

As we have shown in the preceding pages of this
book (pp. 54-69), great solutions were proposed for the
problems created in the wake of the fundamentalist-
modernist controversies of the twenties and thirties;
and, from the perspective of the new evangelical, all
seemed to be going very well, thank you. Going well,
that is, until a significant number of younger men,
converts, trainees and direct descendants of the new
evangelicals decided that their fathers were not
neoevangelical enough. So, they threw over the traces,
as it were.

In *The Young Evangelicals,* Quebedeaux's criticisms
center mainly around the National Association of
Evangelicals, Billy Graham and *Christianity Today.*
These, he insists, constitute the three most important
symbols of Establishment Evangelicalism in America
today.[1]

In summary of his criticism and rejection of
neoevangelicalism and his reason for wishing to be
classified as a young evangelical, he wrote:

> In Establishment Evangelicalism, we have
> discerned an honest effort to break away from the
> separatist impulse and social unconcern of Fun-
> damentalism. The endeavors of those who first
> called themselves Evangelicals are worthy of
> praise in this respect. But we have also seen that
> Establishment Evangelicalism's rejection of
> separatism in principle has not led to a meaningful
> outreach to Christians of other persuasions, nor
> has it brought about any *significant* unity (institu-

tional *or* spiritual) within a deeply divided Chris-
tendom. Furthermore, we have found social concern among Establishment Evangelicals to be often
merely an offering of pious words rather than a
demonstration of prophetic action. Hence, if we
are looking for a powerful expression of spiritual
renewal in Orthodox Christianity—one genuinely
committed to reconciliation and active faith in a
secular society—we shall have to search
elsewhere.[2]

It should be added, many of the early pioneers of
neoevangelicalism are not proud of their offspring represented by Quebedeaux. He and his kind have gone
much too far to the left for them. When they called
originally for a rejection of fundamentalism, they did
not mean that much of a rejection. When they called for
a new kind of evangelicalism, they did not mean that
new. The fact is that many of those who were once
proud to be called neoevangelicals and later new evangelicals now no longer appreciate the labels. Today
there is a so-called right wing and left wing within
neoevangelicalism, and, of course, there are also those
who claim to be in center field.

The present rift within the neoevangelical fold
began over the doctrine of Scripture. It began in the
sixties (see p. 85) and has continued to widen today.
There is a wide chasm within neoevangelicalism between those who believe in the total inerrancy of all
Scripture and those who believe Scripture is liable to
error and, in fact, contains errors in those teachings
which are not central to its purpose. In consequence of
the division over inerrancy, a number of other problems have arisen which further serve to divide the
evangelical world.

Before dealing with the resultant doctrinal departures, I want to set the inerrancy debate clearly before
the reader.[3]

Two recent books reveal clearly the warfare over
the Word of God among would-be evangelicals. The
first of these, *The Battle for the Bible*, was written by

Harold Lindsell while he was editor of *Christianity Today*. The second, a response to Lindsell's book, is entitled *Biblical Authority* and was edited by Jack Rogers of Fuller Theological Seminary.

As these books reveal, two very different views of the extent of the Bible's inspiration are held by those who claim to be evangelical. The fact is this dual view now being publicized has been true for some time (see pp. 73-88).

As early as 1956 neoevangelicals were calling for a "re-opening of the subject of biblical inspiration."[4] At that time the intention was reviewed as "just a pebble in the pond of conservative theology" which "could expand to the bombshell of mid-century evangelicalism."[5] As we now know, that is precisely what has taken place.

In his foreword to *The Battle for the Bible*, Harold J. Ockenga acknowledged these two prominent views regarding the Bible:

> The first view considers all of Scripture to be inspired and true, including the historical, geographical, and scientific teaching. The second view holds that only the Bible teaching on salvation-history and doctrine is true. The Bible is authoritative for faith and practice only. Some who adopt the second view would say that the Bible is plenarily inspired, but that God intended the writers to use their limited knowledge—which is erroneous—in making nonrevelatory statements.[6]

That the evangelical world is being fragmented and divided more and more over the Bible, its self-claimed source of authority, is not a secret. In Lindsell's controversial book he confirms this.

> Fundamentalists and evangelicals (both of whom have been traditionally committed to an infallible or inerrant Scripture) have long been noted for their propagation and defense of an infallible Bible. But more recently, among those who call themselves evangelicals, there has been a marked departure from the viewpoint held by them for so

long. More and more organizations and individuals historically committed to an infallible Scripture have been embracing and propagating the view that the Bible has errors in it. This movement away from the historic standpoint has been most noticeable among those often labeled neo-evangelicals. This change of position with respect to the infallibility of the Bible is widespread and has occurred in evangelical denominations, Christian colleges, theological seminaries, publishing houses, and learned societies.[7]

What Is Meant by a Totally Inerrant Bible?

It may be well to state both positive and negative aspects of what we mean when we say we believe in the total inerrancy of Scripture.

On the positive side, the total inerrancy of the Bible means it does not lie; it does not make mistakes in any of its affirmations. Scripture possesses the quality of absolute freedom from error in all its pronouncements. None of the Bible's statements are contrary to fact. The human writers of Scripture recorded accurately, precisely, what the Holy Spirit desired them to write—no more and no less.

Does this view of Scripture demand word-for-word agreement in parallel passages? No, it only means that each account must tell the truth. Does this view mean that every word of the Bible was dictated by God to the writers? No, there is too much evidence of differences in style among the writers. And yet it is true that considerable portions of the Bible were dictated directly by God. Are there no errors recorded in the Bible? someone asks. Indeed there are. Mistakes are recorded while the record is without mistakes. To what does total inerrancy apply? Does it extend to translations and versions? No, it applies only to the original autographs of Scripture. They were the product of the creative breath of God.

True, we do not have those originals and therefore they cannot be used to prove they are either inerrant or errant. What we do have, though, in the many copies of those originals is the Word of God insofar as it approximates the autographs. And, of course, if the original autographs were not altogether inerrant, what hope have we that in our English Bibles we have the Word of God? What about the many copies of these originals upon which our English Bibles are based? Edward J. Young asks the question and answers it beautifully:

> Are these copies, however, hopelessly corrupt? For our part we are convinced they are not. We believe that the Bible which we have is accurate and that it is a remarkably close approximation to the original manuscripts.
>
> Suppose that a school teacher writes a letter to the president of the United States. To her great joy, she receives a personal reply. It is a treasure which she must share with her pupils and so she dictates the letter to them. They are in the early days of their schooling and spelling is not yet one of their strong points. In his copy of the letter, Johnny has misspelled a few words. Mary has forgotten to cross her t's and to dot her i's. Billy has written one or two words twice. Peter has omitted a word now and then. Nevertheless, despite all these flaws, about thirty copies of the president's letter had been made. Unfortunately, the teacher misplaces the original and cannot find it. To her great sorrow, it is gone. She does not have the copy which came directly from the president's pen. She must be content with those that the little children have made.
>
> Will anyone deny that she has the word of the president? Does she not have his message in just those words in which he wrote it to her? True enough, there are some minor mistakes in the letters, but the teacher may engage in the science of textual criticism and correct them. She may correct the misspelled words and she may write in those words which have been omitted, cross out those which are superfluous. Without any serious difficulty, she may indeed restore the original.[8]

Does a belief in the total inerrancy of the Bible mean that there are no difficulties in the Bible? No, indeed it does not. We must distinguish between a difficulty and a contradiction, however. There are difficulties and seeming contradictions. But since the Bible claims to come from God Who cannot lie, we believe Him and we seek to solve those difficulties. Because we cannot solve every problem in the Bible does not mean there is no solution to that problem. More and more, the problems in Scripture are being solved all the time. There are no new problems which contemporary critics have discovered and, what is more, valid solutions have been offered long ago for the existing problems.[9] When we come upon a problem or an apparent contradiction in the Bible for which we do not have a satisfactory solution, we wait in faith, believing what God has told us about His Word.

The belief in a totally inerrant Bible is based on the Bible's own claims for itself (i.e., 2 Tim. 3:16, 17; 2 Pet. 1:19-21), including those of the Savior (i.e., Matt. 5:17, 18; John 10:34, 35). Those who do not believe in the total inerrancy of Scripture do not begin with its claims, but rather with the phenomena of Scripture. They begin with the problems they see in the Bible and with unbelieving and unsympathetic views and then develop a view of the Bible which allows for errors.

Why Is a Totally Inerrant Bible Rejected Today?

Unfortunately, the belief that the Bible is not totally inerrant is spreading among evangelicals. Liberals, of course, as we would expect, have always believed it. From the beginning they rejected the Bible's inerrancy because they rejected its inspiration. They were at least consistent in that. After all, a book which is not God-breathed surely will not be without error.

Disbelief in the inerrancy of Scripture is rather new among evangelicals. Why? That is the question. Have there been some new discoveries to discredit the Bible? No. Are there some new problems for which there are no satisfactory solutions? No.

Evangelicals who reject the total inerrancy of the Bible do so because they feel the view does not take seriously enough the human side of Scripture.

> Biblical literalism is rejected to the point that evolution, no less than feminism, can be harmonized with the Scriptures. The Bible may indeed be the word of God, but it is also the word of human writers, and it bears the marks of cultural conditioning. Thus older concepts of inerrancy and infallibility are being interpreted in such a way as to focus on the biblical message of salvation rather than on the text itself. For many evangelicals of the left, the appropriate word to describe the Bible is *authoritative,* not infallible or inerrant.[10]

Over and over again we hear it from those who reject total inerrancy: Since the writers of Scripture were human, error is possible in what they wrote which was not directly revealed to them by God. In response it must be said that the same sinful humanity touched all of Scripture. On what basis, therefore, may we be sure that anything they wrote is free from error? The usual answer is: When the human penmen of Scripture wrote what was directly revealed to them about the central theme and purpose of Scripture, they wrote inerrantly. And what, we ask, is the central theme and purpose of Scripture? Salvation and Christian life, is the answer. And who decides when matters of Scripture are central and when they are peripheral? And the embarrassing answer must be the interpreter of Scripture. From those who embrace a totally inerrant Bible, the response comes loud and clear that that is far too subjective and we prefer to let the Bible speak for itself.

> If Scripture itself professes to be inerrant only with respect to revelational or salvatory truth, where is the evidence for this to be found? Not in Scripture. For when the Word of God speaks of its truthwor-

thiness, at no point does it include any limitation. Nor does it indicate that some parts of Scripture are thus to be trusted and other parts are not. If there is any doctrine of infallibility based upon the biblical data, it must include all of Scripture or none of it.[11]

I am convinced that one basic reason underlies all the other reasons for the rejection of the inerrancy of the Bible among neoevangelicals. That reason is related to the attempt to accommodate the Bible to science, falsely so-called, and modern unbelieving scholarship. The rejection is an evidence of the tendency to succumb to the worship of intellectualism and thereby to fail to take God at His Word. This does not mean that those who hold such a view of Scripture are not sincere. Many of them have no doubt embraced their view in answer to honest inquiry. But the fact remains that underlying the initial rejection was usually the attempt to embrace a less objectional view of the Bible, one that would be more harmonious with a naturalist world view.

Why Is It So Important To Hold to a Totally Inerrant Bible?

God cannot lie. To reject what He has said about His Word is to accuse Him of falsehood. How can an errant Bible be God's revelation? How can it be God-breathed? How could it possibly be authoritative and therefore trustworthy? No, God does not lead men astray. To reject a totally inerrant Scripture is to cast aspersions on the very character of God. God's Word and His character are at stake in this debate.

How can Scripture possibly be inerrant in some parts and errant in others at the same time? In a book which claims God as its author, inspiration must extend to all its parts. If it does not, how does one go about determining what is and what is not God-breathed and therefore free from error? If some of it is inerrant, why is not all of it since the revelational and nonrevelational matters were touched by the same human frailty? An errant, inspired Bible is a meaningless designation. An errant Bible which claims to be God's Word is biblically, theologically and philosophically indefensible.

In a general way, every scriptural claim for inspiration is also a claim for inerrancy. There can be no mistaking it: the Savior believed in a totally inerrant Bible. He made no distinction between central and peripheral issues, between scientific and salvation matters. For Him, all of Scripture constituted the inerrant Word of God.[12]

Bible believers do not worship the Bible as often accused, but they do worship the God of the Bible. They believe what He said about the Bible is just as true as what He said about His Son. He can be trusted! Lovers of the Book also cling to what God's Son the Savior said about the Bible. They believe Him too! In fact, these people think it highly inconsistent and well-nigh inexplicable that anyone should say he accepts the Savior for all He claims to be but not what He said about the Scripture.

Believers in the totally inerrant written Word of God are fully cognizant that the ones whom the Spirit chose to write that Word were fully human. Not for a moment do they think the human penmen were sinless either. But along with this belief in the humanity of the writers, they also affirm that the same Spirit Who chose men to write, supernaturally kept them from all error or omission in all that they wrote.

NOTES

1. Richard Quebedeaux, *The Young Evangelicals* (New York: Harper & Row, Publishers, 1974), p. 32.

2. Ibid., p. 37.

3. The remainder of the material in this chapter has been taken in part from Robert Lightner, *The Saviour and the Scripture—*

A Case for Biblical Inerrancy (Grand Rapids: Baker Book House, 1978).

4. "Is Evangelical Theology Changing?" *Christian Life* (March 1956), p. 17.

5. Ibid.

6. Harold Lindsell, *The Battle for the Bible* (Grand Rapids: Zondervan Publishing House, 1976), p. 9.

7. Ibid., p. 20.

8. Edward J. Young, *Thy Word Is Truth* (Grand Rapids: Wm. B. Eerdmans Publishing Co., 1967), p. 57.

9. John W. Haley, *An Examination of the Alleged Discrepancies of the Bible* (Nashville: Nashville Gospel Advocate Co., 1967).

10. Richard Quebedeaux, *The Worldly Evangelicals* (New York: Harper & Row, Publishers, 1978), pp. 98, 99.

11. Lindsell, *The Battle for the Bible*, p. 32.

12. See Lightner, *The Saviour and the Scripture—A Case for Biblical Inerrancy*.

2

Resultant Departures

IN THE PREVIOUS chapter we were introduced to the Young Evangelicals, the Radical Evangelicals. Richard Quebedeaux identifies himself with those whom he often refers to as "Evangelicals to the Left." Obviously if there is a left, there must be a center and a right. Quebedeaux's *The Worldly Evangelicals* is devoted almost entirely to the evangelicals he sees in the center and right of center. He contrasts and compares those in these positions with his own position.

First there were the neoevangelicals who said the fundamentalists tried so hard not to be worldy that they were other-worldly. It wasn't long until the descendants of those early neoevangelicals wished to leave home. They were dissatisfied with the way things were going and were not going. They called themselves the Young Evangelicals and called their parents Establishment Evangelicals. Now, after just a very short time, one of the foremost leaders among them calls them the Worldly Evangelicals, and he is the same one who, four years before, said they were not nearly worldly enough.

Before calling attention to some of the recent doctrinal departures which are closely associated with the

denial of inerrancy, we need to identify the Young
Evangelicals.

Evangelicals to the Left Identified

We noted earlier that many of the descendants of early neoevangelicals are totally dissatisfied with the progress its leaders have made. Neoevangelicals, we saw, have become "Establishment Evangelicalism." Speaking of the neoevangelicals of the 1940s, 50s and 60s, Quebedeaux said: "They appropriated the name evangelical for themselves alone and were recognized as *the evangelicals* by both the liberal religious media and the secular public. It is this particular subculture, which I have termed the evangelical establishment, that is collapsing."[1] He explained why it is collapsing. "The credit or blame can be given largely to the young evangelicals, highly visible Christians who, since 1970, began to identify with the groups that had been excluded by the evangelical establishment."[2]

According to Quebedeaux, the first major recognition and impact of the Young Evangelicals came at the InterVarsity Christian Fellowship-sponsored Urbana '70.[3] And then he classifies InterVarsity Christian Fellowship, Youth for Christ, Young Life, World Vision International and other organizations as evangelical left.[4] Some are more left than others, but all have evangelical left sympathies. He states:

> . . . The vanguard of the evangelical left is centered on a small, highly literate, zealous, and generally younger elite, many of whose spokespersons helped formulate the Chicago Declaration.[5] Evangelicals of the left range from moderate Republicans to democratic socialists, if not Marxists. Most affirm the nuclear family but are at the same time open to alternative . . . lifestyles, from extended families to communes. Just about all of the left evangelicals are feminists and support the ordination of women, egalitarian marriage, and the use of inclusive language. The old evangelical taboos against alcohol, tobacco, social dancing, and the like are almost

universally condemned (as binding, at least). Biblical criticism, used constructively and devoutly, is employed by a great many evangelical students and scholars of the left. They recognize the marks of cultural conditioning on Scripture, and their study of the Bible is informed by their knowledge of the natural, social, and behavioral sciences. Within the evangelical community as a whole, evangelicals of the left are probably a small minority at the present time, but an increasingly vocal and influential one, to say the least.[6]

Departures from Biblical and traditional orthodox beliefs among the radical evangelical left stem from the rejection of the total inerrancy of Scripture. As will be seen, some who do not wish to be called evangelicals of the left nevertheless either hold the same view of Scripture or come dangerously close to holding it. Continued and increased departures in selective crucial areas of doctrine will now be highlighted. A reminder: These should not surprise us in light of a weak view of Scripture. What follows are in addition to embracing a less than totally inerrant Bible. Read again the prophetic remarks of Harold Lindsell as quoted on pages 84 and 85.

The Gospel

More and more the gospel and the task of evangelism are said to include more than the good news that Christ died in the sinner's place. It includes more, we are told, than receiving forgiveness of sin by God's grace through faith in Christ. "Thus, in the minds of the Young Evangelicals, evangelism must reach the *whole* person—his spiritual needs, yes; but also his life in corporate society, his relationship with other men and women and the social structures they create for themselves."[7]

The Young Evangelicals insist that all three—conversion to Christ, discipleship for Christ and social concern—are inseparably linked in the gospel message. They chide Billy Graham for not including more emphasis on societal ills and opposition to the status quo in government in his messages. He speaks about social action and the cause of discipleship, they say, but goes on supporting the political establishment.

> Graham not only fails to condemn American corporate sin with the same vigor that he condemns personal sin, but he frequently identifies with that American system which creates so much evil in the world. This is seen most explicitly in his "Honor America" speech at the Lincoln Memorial, Washington D.C., July 4, 1970. Seven reasons for honoring America were given.[8]

Radical evangelicals believe any message which does not include in it demands for social and political changes is but half the gospel. Interestingly, they see in the message of Leighton Ford, Graham's assistant and probable successor, similarity to their own views. Graham, they believe, once also held a similar view but was so far ahead of his evangelical constituency that he had to change. Ford, however, gives them a sign of hope. He is to them an encouraging development in mass evangelism.

The Young Evangelicals base their view of Leighton Ford on the way he conducts crusades, what he says in his messages, and what he has written. Ford wrote, for example, "Again, compassionate social action should not be confused with evangelism; neither should it be separated from it. Like love and marriage, they go together."[9]

"Leighton Ford, Inter-Varsity Christian Fellowship, and Christian World Liberation Front are three prominent exponents of the new kind of evangelism exposed [sic] by the Young Evangelicals—one that meets the needs of the *whole* person."[10]

Another Young Evangelical raised and answered the question of how to do evangelism.

> In particular how do we do biblical evangelism? Jesus' way was to call persons to repentance and discipleship. That was at the center of His ministry and it must be the center of ours. Calling people to repentance is the most political act anyone can undertake, and until we "politicized"

Christians realize that, our politics will be terribly inadequate.[11]

In 1973 an early spokesman for the Young Evangelicals sounded the same note. "Moreover, a renewed evangelicalism must not hesitate to apply the gospel to the whole of life, to the political and economic as well as the private, personal spheres."[12]

Sounding as it were a word of caution and concern, though admittedly on the side of the Young Evangelicals, Quebedeaux confessed, "Indeed, we can discern very little, if any, reference to heaven and hell (except existentially) in young evangelical publications. Building a just society and developing ethical living here and now seem far more important than preparing people for heaven."[13]

The same writer came very close to saying universalism was creeping into evangelicalism. He based his finds on an article in *Eternity*, December 1976, written by Clark Pinnock. In the article Pinnock insisted that either at death or in some other way God will save those who never heard the gospel and therefore never trusted Christ, but who had nevertheless sought after God.

> Young evangelical activists, who rarely speak of heaven and hell, are reinterpreting the task of evangelism so that it looks to the casual observer more like the call to social justice and peace than the traditional call to conversion, personal regeneration through Christ. . . .
> Finally, the new willingness of many evangelical academics, pastors, and activists to have fellowship and engage in cooperative activities with Protestant liberals (who may deny some of the cardinal tenets of orthodoxy) and Jews, without trying to convert them, makes it difficult to believe that these same evangelicals regard their not born-again colleagues as hell-bound sinners. Clearly, in the minds of such evangelicals, the boundaries between saved and lost have been obscured.[14]

Those who gave birth to neoevangelicalism were not able to hold the line in this area either. Witness the words from a sympathizer, one on the inside.

> And the Karl Barth Society has so many applications for membership from evangelicals that it doesn't know what to do with them. (Strange goings on for leaders of a movement that ten years ago considered neo-orthodoxy and its theologians almost as dangerous as liberalism.) Clearly and undisputedly, the evangelical left is far closer to Bonhoeffer, Brunner, and Barth than to the Hodges and Warfield on the inspiration and authority of Scripture. And it may not be surprising if, despite David Hubbard's words to the contrary, Fuller Seminary eventually becomes the leading center of neo-orthodox conviction in the world—both in theology and in the critical study of Scripture.[15]

Gerald T. Sheppard, assistant professor of Old Testament at Union Theological Seminary wrote of the trends toward neoorthodoxy at Fuller and other seminaries. "Despite all of Hubbard's arguments to the contrary, Fuller as well as most of the seminaries which Lindsell regards as truly 'evangelical,' are no longer in united opposition to neoorthodoxy."[16] Sheppard insisted that the rhetoric used still supports a sharp distinction between "evangelical" and "neoorthodox," but in practice there is little distinction. He feels there is a close association of evangelicalism as represented by the Young Evangelicals with neoorthodoxy.[17]

Donald Dayton, assistant professor of theology at North Park Theological Seminary, went so far as to call George Ladd's view expressed in his *The New Testament and Criticism* "a largely neoorthodox position."[18]

There is no question about it, the Evangelicals of the Left have gone far beyond including neoevangelicals in evangelistic campaigns, like Graham has done for years. Those to the left are far removed from the old fundamentalist-modernist struggles. They have been taught that the battle is over. They "see no reason not to consider the possibility of relating to mainline Protestants as equals—sisters and brothers in Christ. . . . Left evangelicals have been courted by the NCC and the WCC, mainline Protestant church bureaucrats, major ecumenical and denonimational campus ministry organizations, and a number of prominent liberal theological seminaries."[19]

Personal Separation

Throughout most of *The Young Evangelicals*, fundamentalists as well as evangelicals who take the apostle John seriously when he tells believers not to love the world or the things in it (1 John 2:15) are ridiculed and made fun of. Any who have convictions against things which many modern evangelicals see no harm in are considered legalists.

> The Young Evangelicals insist that many forms of cultural participation may indeed be legitimate for Christians—e.g., moderate drinking, card-playing, social dancing, listening to rock music, and attendance at the theater—despite the fact that these have been traditionally banned by the majority of Evangelicals and Fundamentalists. In fact, they feel that such activities *can* be understood as God's good gifts for the use (not misuse) of his children.[20]

Neither are Young Evangelicals alone in this downplay of the doctrine of personal separation from the world and the things which promote its anti-God philosophy.

> An increasing number of evangelicals—left, center and right—no longer consider the traditional revivalistic taboos to be mandatory. When young people were converted in the Jesus movement, many of them simply did not give up their former habits, practices, and cultural attitudes— drinking, smoking, and characteristic dress and language. They only modified them. Evangelicals often discovered the pleasure of alcohol and tobacco while studying and traveling in Europe, where the typical revivalistic taboos do not func-

tion among local evangelical and charismatic Christians. Young evangelicals drink, but so do conservative evangelicals like Hal Lindsey and John Warwick Montgomery (who is a member of the International Wine and Food Society). Many young evangelicals smoke (a pipe, especially), but so does Jacob Preus, president of The Lutheran Church—Missouri Synod. In addition, four-letter and other once-proscribed words are now common in the conversation of left evangelicals. . . .

It should be said at this point, however, that left evangelicals do tend to be more moderate in their behavior in all these areas than their Protestant liberal, Roman Catholic, and secular counterparts. There is clearly less drunkenness among them, and they are generally reluctant to use drugs. But even marijuana, now virtually legal in some areas of the United States, is not as forbidden among young evangelicals as it once was. A few of them, particularly the intellectuals, do smoke it on occasion, despite the fact that dope smoking is still discouraged by leaders of the evangelical left as a whole.[21]

In reality the life-style of growing numbers of those who claim to be evangelical is little different from the unregenerate. The professed believer may not do things to the same excess as the unbeliever. The differences are mostly of degree, however, and not of kind. Once the world's philosophy is embraced, or even viewed with respect, its practices soon follow.

Feminists

There is an "evangelical feminism" (often called "biblical feminism"), as well as a secular women's liberation movement. It is a movement closely associated with the evangelical left. According to one sympathetic to the movement, it may be traced to Russell Prohl's book *Women in the Church*, published in 1957 by Eerdmans. Later articles in *Eternity* (February 1966 and 1968) by Letha Scanzoni, advocated the ordination of women. In 1974 Nancy Hardesty and Scanzoni co-authored *All We're Meant To Be: A Biblical Approach to*

194

Women's Liberation. [22] This gave a tremendous boost to the movement.

The signers of the Chicago Declaration (see note 5, p. 197), admitted: ". . . We have encouraged men to prideful domination and women to irresponsible passivity. So we call both men and women to mutual submission and active discipleship."[23] By "mutual submission" Young Evangelical feminists mean "equality," used so commonly by secular feminists today.

At an Evangelical Feminists Conference in Washington, D.C., in November 1975 the Equal Rights Amendment was endorsed. Leaders among the feminists insist that they believe the Bible but do not believe it teaches concerning women what it has been said to teach. Without doubt these feminists find much support from Paul K. Jewett's *Man as Male and Female* (Eerdmans, 1975). The Fuller Theological Seminary professor simply considers Paul and other writers of Scripture to have erred when they made particular pointed statements which appear to contradict the general foundational truths of human equality. Quebedeaux rightly summarized Jewett's view in these words:

> . . . Jewett believes that Paul's teachings about women (except Galatians 3:28) were influenced both by his male-dominated culture and by rabbinic traditions representing no more than a time-bound authority, not applicable to later Christians in other cultures. When we discern the cultural conditionings of Scripture, we are also free to say that a writer, like Paul, may indeed be wrong at points.[24]

Virginia Ramey Mollenkott, an associate of *The Other Side,* a radical evangelical publication, also lends support to evangelical feminists. She, too, believes Paul to be self-contradictory. "Only in the past six months have I been willing to state which this Pauline self-contradiction says to me, and it's with fear and trembling that I do."[25] After making this statement, Mollenkott wrote of her departure from her Plymouth Brethren background and the encouragement she received from

Paul K. Jewett and Letha Scanzoni. She then said, "Now I get to the problem. The inter-testamental rabbinic misogyny is the background against which Paul must be read. Paul was trained by Gamalial, one of the most famous of rabbis. As a man socialized in the very chauvenistic society, naturally Paul would believe in the inferiority of women."[26]

It is not difficult to see how a weak view of Scripture led easily to this deviation and departure from the Biblical teaching of the role of women in the home and the church.

The Charismatic Movement

Relational theology is common among the evangelical left. We can probably best understand it by contrasting it with revelational theology. The latter is doctrine derived from the revealed Word of God. The former represents beliefs based upon experiences and relationships with others. It rests upon the subjective rather than the objective. As we might suspect, the Young Evangelicals are strong on relational theology. This emphasis is clearly evident in the writings of men like Keith Miller and Bruce Larson, for example.[27]

The emphasis on relational theology sets the stage beautifully for sympathy and cooperation with the Charismatic Renewal Movement.

> Numerous New Evangelical thinkers and Young Evangelicals are attracted to that unity. Some even share the Charismatic experience and are involved in various institutions and organizations associated with the Neo-Pentecostalism—Oral Roberts University, Full Gospel Business Men's Fellowship International, the Kathryn Kuhlman ministry, Melodyland Christian Center in Anaheim, California, and the like. Perhaps Charismatic Renewal and the Young Evangelicals can continue to learn from each other, and even complement one another in their mutual quest for spiritual renewal and a whole Gospel relevant to every dimension of life.[28]

Where will the continued liberalizing trends within neoevangelicalism end? Will today's neo-evangelicals be tomorrow's liberals? Many people outside the circle of evangelicalism are not yet aware of the revolution going on within the ranks of evangelicalism. Unfortunately, the same is true even for many on the inside. Thus the need for such a study as this. In view of the rapid changes which have taken place, one cannot help but ask, Where will it all end?

Even Quebedeaux admitted with some alarm the continued liberalizing tendencies.

> . . . I am not quite as optimistic and uncritical in treating the evangelical left as I was five years ago. At that time I assumed that evangelicals could be genuinely faithful to the Gospel (and "progressive") only insofar as they became more like—but not too much like—liberals. However, now that this liberalizing tendency among evangelicals is readily apparent and growing, I'm no longer certain that it's a good thing at all.[29]

Robert S. Ellwood, Jr. of the School of Religion at the University of Southern California gave his evaluation of the expressions of revolution within evangelicalism.

> Is the new evangelicalism . . . really something new *within* evangelicalism, or is [it] the shaky, searching first steps of a reborn liberalism? For while the new evangelicals avoid like the plague any language suggestive of mature "social gospel," "modernist," or "secular theology" liberalism, their theology on basic points like the meaning of Scripture seems to involve some subtle shifts in the direction of the seminal liberalism of Schleiermacher, Maurice, or Bushnell. I wondered if history were not repeating itself rather than doing something new . . . perhaps paralleling the well-known changes in rhetoric and style that evangelical churches like the Methodist underwent several generations ago as their constituencies moved up the education and affluence ladders.[30]

I conclude with this honest appraisal of the evangelical left by one who admits he holds that position and to whom we have referred often in these chapters.

> . . . The evangelical left provides a better option [better than liberalism] for evangelicals who may still *believe* like evangelicals, but wish to *behave* like liberals. Furthermore, among this group there may be an increasingly large number of people who really *have* moved beyond evangelical belief toward liberalism. In other words, they have rejected the evangelical position intellectually (though they may not admit or even recognize it), but they still have an *emotional* attachment to the movement in which they were converted and nurtured. This unfortunate stance is especially characteristic of a number of graduates of left evangelical seminaries (like Fuller), who were reared in conservative denominations and homes, affiliated with a mainline denomination while in seminary (like The United Presbyterian Church in the U.S.A.), and became pastor or associate pastor of a liberal congregation in that denomination. Thus some evangelicals *are* becoming liberals without saying so. But it is still too early to discern where this current trend will lead.[31]

NOTES

1. Quebedeaux, *The Worldly Evangelicals*, p. 22.
2. Ibid., pp. 23, 24.
3. Ibid., p. 83.
4. Ibid., pp. 101-114.
5. The following is from a review of *The Chicago Declaration* by Ronald J. Sider (Carol Stream, IL: Creation House, 1974) which appeared in *Bibliotheca Sacra* (April—June 1975). The book represents the story behind the November 23, 1973, meeting in Chicago of about fifty evangelicals who met to wrestle with evangelical social concerns. "It wanted to include both Northerners and Southerners, both evangelical, elder statesmen, and younger more 'radical' evangelical voices" (p. 22).

Foy Valentine, executive secretary of the Southern Baptist Convention Christian Life Commission, spelled out in his paper one of the goals of the Chicago meeting. "Many Christians are becoming angry at those within the churches who agitate for action and press for social change. These believe there is no place in the church for social concern. They want the Bible preached in the truncated form to which they have become accustomed and the culture religion of our established churches. They would abolish our work and obliterate our emphasis from the church's life. . . . These radical individualists view religion as purely personal and the church's task is that of providing preaching, Bible study, and soul-saving service. They hold that on their own initiative saved souls may then define whatever avenues they can to do what God may want done in the world. Our task is to convert these *modernists* who have turned away from Moses and the prophets, and from Paul, John, Peter and James, and from Jesus to embrace that wretched false and abominable misleading dualism which never ceases to plague the Christian church" (pp. 61, 62).

The whole thrust of the meeting was that "evangelism and social action are inseparable" (p. 30). Fundamentalists and older evangelicals were accused of preaching the gospel void of any social concern. That seems a bit strange to this reviewer in light of the fact that the meeting was held only a stone's throw from the Pacific Garden Mission, which was certainly not started by "younger," "radical" evangelicals.

For my part the emphasis of the Chicago meeting was upon social change as a primary role of the church with only lip service paid to the gospel as Paul knew it and preached it. As I read the book I couldn't help but wonder why Jesus didn't say and do more about all the social injustices of His day. Why didn't He make social concern His primary objective? Had He been at the Chicago meeting, I think He would have said, "Preach the gospel as it is in the New Testament and don't try to bring the world into conformity with the church."

6. Quebedeaux, *The Worldly Evangelicals*, p. 84.

7. Quebedeaux, *The Young Evangelicals*, p. 81.

8. Joe Roos, *The Post-American* (Spring 1972), pp. 9, 10, quoted in Quebedeaux, *The Young Evangelicals*, p. 84.

9. Leighton Ford, *One Way to Change the World* (New York: Harper & Row, Publishers, 1970), p. 114, quoted in Quebedeaux, *The Young Evangelicals*, pp. 88, 89.

10. Quebedeaux, *The Young Evangelicals*, p. 97.

11. Jim Wallis, "An Agenda for Tomorrow," *The Other Side* (July—August 1975), p. 48.

12. Donald G. Bloesch, *The Evangelical Renaissance* (Grand Rapids: Wm. B. Eerdmans Publishing Co., 1973), p. 46.

13. Quebedeaux, *The Worldly Evangelicals*, p. 19.

14. Ibid., p. 21.

15. Ibid., p. 100.

16. "Biblical Hermeneutics: The Academic Language of Evangelical Identity," *Union Seminary Quarterly Review*, XXXII (Winter 1977), p. 91.

17. Ibid., p. 94.

18. "Where Now Young Evangelicals?" *The Other Side* (March—April 1976), p. 35.

19. Quebedeaux, *The Worldly Evangelicals*, p. 135.

20. Quebedeaux, *The Young Evangelicals*, p. 133.

21. Quebedeaux, *The Worldly Evangelicals*, pp. 118, 119.

22. Ibid., pp. 121, 122.

23. Ronald J. Sider, *The Chicago Declaration* (Carol Stream, IL: Creation House, 1974), p. 2.

24. Quebedeaux, *The Worldly Evangelicals*, p. 124.

25. *The Other Side* (May—June 1976), pp. 24, 25.

26. Ibid., p. 26.

27. See especially Larson's *Ask Me to Dance* (Waco, TX: Word Books, 1972) and his *The Relational Revelation* (Waco, TX: Word Books, 1976).

28. Quebedeaux, *The Young Evangelicals*, p. 45.

29. Quebedeaux, *The Worldly Evangelicals*, p. xii.

30. Review of *The Worldly Evangelicals* by Richard Quebedeaux, *Anglican Theological Review* (July 1975), pp. 380, 381, quoted by Quebedeaux, *The Worldly Evangelicals*, pp. 165, 166.

31. Quebedeaux, *The Worldly Evangelicals*, pp. 166, 167.

Annotated Bibliography

This bibliography has been prepared primarily for student use. It includes references both favorable and unfavorable to fundamentalism and neoevangelicalism. These sources have been selected out of many because of their peculiar relevance to the contemporary theological scene as it has been discussed in this book.

A. Books

General

Berkhof, L. *Recent Trends in Theology*. Grand Rapids: Wm. B. Eerdmans Publishing Company, 1946. This survey of trends in contemporary theology identifies tendencies and methods which are helpful in understanding neoevangelicalism.

Cobb, John B., Jr. *Varieties of Protestantism*. Philadelphia: The Westminster Press, 1960. Written from a liberal perspective. The author seeks to demonstrate that the nine types of Protestantism which he presents are all Christian types.

DeWolf, L. Harold. *The Case for Theology in Liberal Perspective*. Philadelphia: The Westminster Press,

1959. This presentation of neoliberalism reveals the system with which neoevangelicalism is seeking an audience. DeWolf presents a human subjective basis of authority and a human Christ not able to make a substitutionary atonement.

_____. *Present Trends in Christian Thought*. New York: Association Press, 1960. Though a spokesman for neoliberalism, DeWolf surveys in this small volume the contemporary Protestant scene. The book is easy to read and is quite objective.

Hazelton, Roger. *New Accents in Contemporary Theology*. New York: Harper and Brothers, 1960. An attempt to show the relationship of theology with the arts, the sciences, philosophy, Biblical scholarship, ecumenism and representatives of non-Christian religions.

Hordern, William. *The Case for a New Reformation Theology*. Philadelphia: The Westminster Press, 1959. A clear presentation of the tenets of neoorthodoxy based on the usual neoorthodox presuppositions.

_____. *A Layman's Guide to Protestant Theology*. New York: The Macmillan Company, 1955. The author seeks to interpret theology for the nontechnical reader. He deals with fundamentalism as a defense of orthodoxy and liberalism as that which has remade orthodoxy. Neoorthodoxy is viewed as a rediscovery of orthodoxy.

Lindsell, Harold. *The Battle for the Bible*. Grand Rapids: Zondervan Publishing House, 1976. A detailed exposé of individuals and organizations still claiming to be evangelical but no longer holding to the total inerrancy of Scripture. Fuller Theological Seminary is set forth as Exhibit #1.

Rogers, Jack, ed., *Biblical Authority*. Waco, TX: Word Books, 1977. Both a Fuller Seminary professor and the president join other contributors to respond to *The Battle for the Bible* and to call for the Bible's authority without its total inerrancy.

Soper, David Wesley. *Major Voices in American Theology*. A survey of the lives and writings of contemporary theological thinkers.

ANNOTATED BIBLIOGRAPHY

Fundamentalism

Cole, Stewart G. *The History of Fundamentalism*. New York: Harper and Brothers, 1931. Includes little theological analysis, but it is useful for references to men, organizations and primary sources.

Dollar, George W. *A History of Fundamentalism in America*. Greenville, SC: Bob Jones University Press, 1973. The author distinguishes and identifies militant, moderate and modified fundamentalists.

Feinberg, Charles L., ed. *The Fundamentals for Today*. 2 vols. Grand Rapids: Kregel Publications, 1958. The third publication of *The Fundamentals*. A defense of historic Christianity.

Furniss, Norman J. *The Fundamentalist Controversy, 1918-1931*. Hamden, CT: Archon Books, 1963. No theological analysis, but it is useful for references to men, organizations and primary sources.

Gaspèr, Louis. *The Fundamentalist Movement*. New York: Humanities Press, Inc., 1963. The author stresses what he sees as the contrasts between fundamentalism as represented in the American Council of Christian Churches and that breed of fundamentalism represented in the National Association of Evangelicals. He suggests that the errors of the older, more original fundamentalism are represented by the American Council of Christian Churches and that the National Association of Evangelicals consists of a new breed of fundamentalists whom the author states are referred to as neoevangelicals by their friends and their foes.

Machen, J. Gresham. *Christianity and Liberalism*. New York: The Macmillan Co., 1923. A defense of orthodoxy against the older liberalism.

_____. *What Is Faith?* New York: The Macmillan Co., 1935. The author shows that faith is not a work. It is not doing something, but believing something.

Packer, J. I. *Fundamentalism and the Word of God.* Grand Rapids: Wm. B. Eerdmans Publishing Co., 1959. An attempt to resolve some of the contemporary misunderstandings of fundamentalism, especially as they relate to authority.

Sandeen, Ernest R. *The Roots of Fundamentalism: British and American Millenarianism, 1800-1930.* Chicago: University of Chicago Press, 1970. The subtitle accurately defines the work. The author equates premillennialism with fundamentalism.

Stevick, Daniel B. *Beyond Fundamentalism.* Richmond: John Knox Press, 1964. A bitter attack upon fundamentalism by one who originally espoused it but has gone where the title indicates.

Stott, John R. W. *Fundamentalism and Evangelism.* Grand Rapids: Wm. B. Eerdmans Publishing Co., 1959. A study of the usage of the term *fundamentalism* in England and an appraisal of the Graham crusade there.

Neoevangelicalism

Bloesch, Donald G. *The Evangelical Renaissance.* Grand Rapids: Wm. B. Eerdmans Publishing Co., 1973. The author claims to be "both evangelical and ecumenical" and writes with approval of the new evangelicalism.

Carnell, Edward John. *The Case for Orthodox Theology.* Philadelphia: The Westminster Press, 1959. A polemic against what the author calls "cultic orthodoxy" which he identifies as fundamentalism.

Ferm, Robert O. *Cooperative Evangelism.* Grand Rapids: Zondervan Publishing House, 1958. A defense of the evangelistic efforts of the Billy Graham crusade.

Henry, Carl F. H., ed. *Contemporary Evangelical Thought*. Great Neck, NY: Channel Press, 1957. A survey of the viewpoints of authorities in vital areas of evangelical thought today.

_____. *The Drift of Western Thought*. Grand Rapids: Wm. B. Eerdmans Publishing Co., 1951.

_____. *Evangelical Responsibility in Contemporary Theology*. Grand Rapids: Wm. B. Eerdmans Publishing Co., 1957. A development of the place of evangelicalism in view of the liberal perversion and fundamentalist reduction of Christianity.

_____. *The Protestant Dilemma*. Grand Rapids: Wm. B. Eerdmans Publishing Co., 1949.

_____. *The Uneasy Conscience of Modern Fundamentalism*. Grand Rapids: Wm. B. Eerdmans Publishing Co., 1947. A strong criticism of contemporary fundamentalism.

Kik, Marcellus J. *Ecumenism and the Evangelical*. Philadelphia: The Presbyterian and Reformed Publishing Co., 1958. An effort to relate evangelicalism to the ecumenical movement.

Nash, Ronald H. *The New Evangelicalism*. Grand Rapids: Zondervan Publishing House, 1963. An attempted defense of neoevangelicalism. The author seeks to prove without success that neoevangelicalism is the same as historic fundamentalism.

Orr, James. *The Second Evangelical Awakening in America*. London: Marshall, Morgan and Scott, 1952.

Pickering, Ernest D. *The Fruit of Compromise: The New and Young Evangelicals*. Clarks Summit, PA: Baptist Bible College of Pennsylvania, n.d. A summary of the development and departures of the new and young evangelicals.

Quebedeaux, Richard. *The Worldly Evangelicals*. New York: Harper & Row, Publishers, 1978. An alarming record of how far toward the left those in the center and to the right of center in neoevangelicalism have moved.

──────────. *The Young Evangelicals*. New York: Harper & Row, Publishers, 1974. A bold and critical analysis of neoevangelicalism and fundamentalism by a member of the "evangelical left."

Shelley, Bruce L. *Evangelicalism in America*. Grand Rapids: Wm. B. Eerdmans Publishing Co., 1967. This work gives considerable attention to the National Association of Evangelicals.

Wells, David F. and John D. Woodbridge, eds. *The Evangelicals*. Nashville: Abingdon Press, 1975. Written by those sympathetic to evangelicalism, the book proposes to identify evangelicals, tell what they believe and where they are changing.

Woodbridge, Charles. *The New Evangelicalism*. Greenville, SC: Bob Jones University Press, 1969.

B. Periodical Articles
of Special Significance to Neoevangelicalism

"A Conversation With Young Evangelicals," *The Post-American*, January 1975.

Collins, Gary. "The Pit and the Pendulum," *Eternity*, October 1977.

Dayton, Donald. "Where Now Young Evangelicals?" *The Other Side*, March—April 1975.

"Demythologizing Neo-evangelicalism," *Christian Century*, September 15, 1965.

Didden, Clarence H. "Neo-evangelicalism in the Light of Prophecy," *Biblical Research Monthly*, August 1969.

Hefley, James. "How I Lost My Protestant Prejudice," *Eternity*, November 1971.

Henry, Carl F. H. "A Note to the Young Evangelicals," *Eternity*, November 1975.

──────────. "Agenda for Evangelical Advance," *Christianity Today*, November 5, 1976.

_____. "Conflict Over Biblical Inerrancy," *Christianity Today*, May 7, 1976.

_____. "Evangelical Renewal," *Christianity Today*, June 5, 1973.

_____. "Evangelical Social Concern," *Christianity Today*, March 1, 1974.

_____. "Revolt on the Evangelical Frontier," *Christianity Today*, April 26, 1974.

_____. "Signs of Evangelical Disunity," *Christianity Today*, April 9, 1976.

Hine, Leland D. "Is Evangelicalism Dying of Old Age?" *Eternity*, March 1972.

Kucharsky, David. "The Year of the Evangelical," *Christianity Today*, October 22, 1976.

Lindsell, Harold. "Think of These Things," *Moody Monthly*, October 1975.

McCure, Roland D. "Second Generation New Evangelicals," *Central Biblical Quarterly*, Winter 1974.

McKenna, David L. "Drinking at a Shrinking Water Hole," *United Evangelical Action*, Winter 1975.

Morris, Leon. "Conservative Evangelicalism," *Christianity Today*, November 19, 1971.

Ramm, Bernard L. "Welcome Green-Grass Evangelicals," *Eternity*, March 1974.

Tarr, Leslie K. "The Hermetically-Sealed World of Neo-Fundamentalism," *Eternity*, August 1976.

"Thirty Years of New Evangelicalism," *The Ohio Bible Fellowship Visitor*, December 1976.

Waggonner, John E. "Can Evangelicalism Be Ecumenical?" *Eternity*, December 1971.

C. Unpublished Materials

Grounds, Vernon G. "Fundamentalism and Evangelicalism: Legitimate Labels or Illicit Labels?" Denver: Conservative Baptist Seminary. (Mimeographed.) Definitive of fundamentalism and evangelicalism.

Ketcham, Robert T. "A New Peril in Our Last Days." Chicago: General Association of Regular Baptist Churches. (Mimeographed.) An analysis of "Is Evangelical Theology Changing?" *Christian Life*, March 1956. It is a declaration of the dangers within neoevangelicalism.